# 12 Ways to Fix
# Lath and Plaster Ceilings

Complete Do-it-Yourself Guide for
Homeowners

by

Ian Anderson MSc LCGI

# 12 Ways to Fix
# Lath and Plaster Ceilings

### Complete Do-it-Yourself
### Guide for Homeowners

Published by handycrowd media

Reg No. 995979268 in Norway

## ISBN 978-82-93249-02-3

**Disclaimer:** The author has made every effort to ensure that the information in this book is accurate. However, since it cannot be determined what you intend to do with this information or how competent you are, it shall be your own responsibility to ensure this information meets your specific requirements. The author is a professional builder educated in the UK and the working practices and observations in this book reflect this. It is your responsibility to ensure the advice given in this book is suitable for your country or situation, as working practices and rules differ from country to country. It is your responsibility as the homeowner to ensure you have permission to carry out alterations and additions to your home.

## Seek local professional advice if you are
## in any way unsure.

# CONTENTS

iv

# INTRODUCTION TO LATH AND PLASTER

As a general contractor working predominantly in the UK for more than 30 years, I've worked on more than my fair share of lath and plaster ceilings. From restoring them in period properties, to ripping them out in turn of the century terraced houses and starting afresh with drywall. I've seen many variants, from wonderfully crafted works of art, to awful ones quickly thrown up by 'cheap' industrialists, and even some with reeds instead of laths.

Although I've removed countless lath and plaster ceilings myself, I'm always a little sad when an original ceiling hits the floor in a cloud of dust. I just can't shake the feeling that the house has lost a little of its character and is all the poorer for it. As you can probably tell, I adore lath and plaster for its charming authenticity and skilled construction. Although I might say something slightly different after I've just removed one and I'm totally covered in very old black dust, incorporating the odd mouse skeleton, thrown in for good measure...

However, I hope you love *your* lath and plaster, even if it does give you sleepless nights! Let's go and take a quick look at your ceilings, then we can run through some of the options you have to repair and keep them. Alternatively (and sadly); if needs must, I'll show you how to remove them safely and install new ceilings, either with like for like laths and traditional lime-based plasters, or more commonly, with modern drywall boards and gypsum-based plasters. But first, some housekeeping notes...

**WHAT *IS* LATH AND PLASTER?**

Up to the 1950's before drywall became common, thin wooden laths were nailed to ceiling joists (leaving small gaps in between) and plastered. In the UK, split or riven hardwood* lath was the norm, but sawn timber was common in the USA. The plaster consisted of two coats of a lime/sand haired mortar, followed by a two thin finish coats, trowelled to a smooth, flat surface. The thickness of finished ceilings varied from 19mm (3/4") up to around 28.5mm (1, 1/8$^{th}$). You might find thinner or even thicker sections, especially in older houses built with hand cut joists or those built using recycled materials (spars from old ships etc.).     *oak or chestnut usually.

## WHAT *IS* DRYWALL?

You might be wondering why I'm calling it drywall. Well, I'll use the word *drywall* in this book as a handy 'catch all' term because these boards have many different names in other countries. In the UK, we say *plasterboard* but in New Zealand it's *gib* and in the USA the brand name *sheetrock* is common. Other generic names include baseboard, gyproc, gyprock, gypsum board and wallboard. Moreover, on a building site it's often just 'boards'.

I'm living in Norway these days and here we call it 'gips', derived from gypsum I guess, since all drywall boards consist of a gypsum-based plaster slurry encased in-between two sheets of very thick paper. This creates strong, cheap, and easily worked building boards.

## IS IT LATH OR LATHE?

Lath. End of lesson. In case you're interested a lathe is a machine for turning round bits of metal (or wood) and the plural of lath is laths (although we could probably argue a little about that last one...)

## IS THIS BOOK RELEVANT FOR LATH AND PLASTER WALLS?

Yes indeedy, you'd use the same principles and methods to repair or remove it from walls also. Only it's a little easier to remove because you're not standing directly underneath all the muck!

Plastering on lathed walls is a bit tricky though, as the mortar can easily just drop off the back of the lath as you push it though. Whereas on a ceiling the mortar squeezes through the lath and forms beautiful mushroom shaped keys.

# INSPECTING AND EVALUATING CEILINGS

*In a period house, improvements are often a compromise between originality and practicality, oh and cost...*

Period charm probably led you to buy an older house in the first place; after all, why would you go through the trials and tribulations of owning a gently decaying pile of bricks if not? Along with the soft honey coloured lime mortar and moss-covered roof tiles, your lath and plasterwork undoubtedly adds to the period feel of your home.

Plus, if your home is a highly listed property, your local authority might insist you repair and keep them. However, for the average home, the big question facing most owners is how to find a practical solution that doesn't spoil the very charm and feel that tempted you to buy the house in the first place.

To find a suitable solution though, we have to be pragmatic; accepting that times change and that our needs and expectations change with them. For example, modern recessed light fittings are difficult to fit into a lath and plaster ceiling, at least not without a lot of work, (often you'd need to cut out squares of the lath and plaster and patch them up with small squares of drywall, which is fiddly and time consuming).

Cost is also a major factor for many people when deciding what to do with a damaged ceiling. During initial renovations of a newly acquired house for example, replacing a ceiling with drywall is not that big a hit on the budget. However, repairing and restoring a damaged original ceiling in a 'finished' home is time consuming, more technically difficult to do well and of course more expensive. This prompts many people to remove ceilings (arguably prematurely) as a safeguard against bigger bills in the future.

The case for keeping original ceilings isn't helped by the fact that any competent DIY enthusiast or local tradesman is capable of removing an old ceiling and installing drywall to a good standard relatively cheaply. Whereas unless you're very confident with the 'wet' stuff, you might need to hire in expensive and often difficult to find skilled plasterers to replace a ceiling in a more traditional manner using age appropriate materials.

However, we really are getting ahead of ourselves; replacing ceilings is only one option. Assuming you've got a problem ceiling, or one you're worried about, let's do an inspection first to evaluate its condition and then we can run through some different options.

A small caveat first though OK? As I mentioned before, plaster ceilings in historically valuable houses might *need* repairing rather than removing. Always check with your local authorities planning or building control department to see if there are any restrictions on what you can and can't do with your ceilings. And before you cringe in fear, always remember that listed and historically valuable properties pose a serious financial quandary for most local authorities, because although they bear responsibility for their future, they are often extremely financially limited.

In practice, I find that local conservation officers are *extremely happy* you're going to spend good money on the upkeep and preservation of your fine house. All they ask is that you allow them to steer you in the right direction, ensuring your repairs, maintenance and improvements are appropriate for the long-term well-being and survival of your home. That's not too much to ask is it?

In addition, your local planning officer is usually a treasure trove of useful information about your home and may even be able to help you find local resources, such as suitable (matching) materials or even local artisans sympathetic to working on older properties like yours.

OK, OK, enough of the blurb I hear you cry; lead the way then, take me to your plasterwork...

## INSPECTION

Working from a suitable, sturdy stepladder let's properly inspect your ceiling, because only then can you properly evaluate its condition and answer the tough question, "Is this ceiling repairable or do I have to replace it?"

On a bright day, stand underneath one corner of your ceiling on your stepladder and with your head almost touching the ceiling look across the ceilings surface; do a 90-degree sweep (wall to wall), looking for cracks, sagging sections or unevenness, etc. Repeat from all four corners because the light hits the ceiling differently from each angle and might hide or highlight problems. It's possible your ceiling looks quite flat from the floor, but once you get up close, you'll get a much better idea of its condition. Feel free to hold up a 6' (1.8m) long piece of straight wood or a plasterer's straight edge to get a better idea of where any bumps and dips are (but don't panic if it's not flat, gentle undulations are quite normal, few things are flat in an older house).

Look out for one or more of the following...

- Thin hairline cracks in random patterns across the ceilings surface.

- Larger cracks with small missing pieces alongside.

- Bumps and other evidence of previous repairs over old cracks or damage.

- Patches of missing plasterwork, sometimes exposing areas of the lath (these will be obvious from the floor I know, duh!).

- Cracks around the edges of the room (wall to ceiling).

- Delaminated plaster, either in the thin finish coats or even through the base coats.

- Bellies or dips in the ceiling, caused by sagging areas of plasterwork (broken keys).

- Bellies across the whole ceiling caused by sagging joists (not always disastrous).

- Thick flaking layers of paint (on neglected ceilings).

Where you see cracks or sagging areas, stand underneath and gently push upwards with the palms of your hands. A tiny amount of give is normal, but if you can actually feel the plaster move up and down (often accompanied by a faint crunching or grinding noise), this means the plaster has separated from the laths (broken keys). A little dust and debris may fall from any cracks as you do this.

NOTE: Please, please, please don't go crazy here! If you push and shove a badly damaged ceiling really hard, you might end up 'wearing' it, literally! Go gently my friend; you're only trying to see if the plaster has separated from the lath, you're not auditioning for a role in the next Avengers movie...

Another useful thing you can do on lower floors is to get someone (preferably a big chap!) to walk around upstairs whilst you watch the ceiling and especially any cracks for excessive movement. If there is a poor joist that's flexing over a crack it's going to be near impossible to repair, as it will just crack again because of the flexing load from above.

NOTE: If the joists are flexing because of damage (rot/insect/etc.), you'll need to replace them. Either individually 'one by one', or by removing the whole floor if that's an option. If the joists are flexing because they are undersized in a poorly constructed place, you'll need to replace them with wider, stiffer ones or even deeper ones (if you have a little headroom to spare...).

## IT'S ALL ABOUT THE KEYS

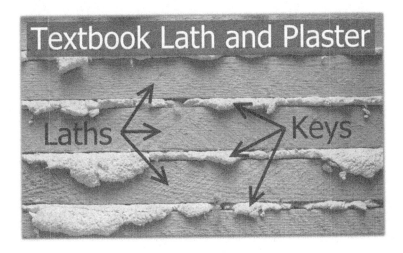

Plaster literally hangs underneath the laths from curls of plaster that have squeezed through gaps in between the laths. These curls, called keys (or sometimes nibs or snots) are *vital* to the integrity of the plasterwork. Lath nails rarely actually fail and it's usually broken plaster keys which allow a ceilings plasterwork to sag down.

If possible, inspect a worrisome ceiling from above, as this is the best way to determine if a significant number of keys have broken off, allowing the plaster to sag. Usually you'll access the top of a ceiling by lifting out loft insulation on the top floor or by removing floorboards on lower levels.

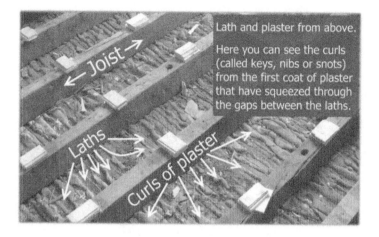

Lath and plaster from above.

Here you can see the curls (called keys, nibs or snots) from the first coat of plaster that have squeezed through the gaps between the laths.

In the pic above you can clearly see the ceiling underneath is in good shape with most of the plaster keys still intact and nicely curled over the laths. I thought that wasn't too shabby for a house built in 1722... (I know, actually pretty amazing huh?)

You'll probably find some broken keys though; it's fairly inevitable after all this time, but as long as the majority are still firm, the plasters structural integrity could still be good. If there's a lot of debris covering up the keys, gently, and I mean really, *really* gently, clear it away using a paintbrush or a brush attachment on a shop vacuum cleaner (on a mild-power setting). On no account, scrape anything, *ever*. The keys are really quite fragile, even when in great shape. Work like an archaeologist who's just discovered the find of a lifetime...

## EVALUATION

Ok, now you've had a good look at your ceiling and you might have spotted a couple of things that worry you. Let's start by looking at what typically causes damage and whether the problem is ongoing or old and static. Here are some common causes of ceiling problems...

## SETTLEMENT

Old houses settle and move around, taking the ceilings along for the ride. A shift in the foundations caused by an unusually cold winter, or a record-breaking summer, or even when the drains clogged with roots and burst (washing away part of the foundations), might have twisted the whole house a little. This slow twisting causes pressure or stress to build up in the relatively thin plaster on the ceiling, eventually cracking it at the weakest points.

However, a crack or two doesn't necessarily spell the end; it's quite possible the plaster is still firmly attached to the lath on both sides of the crack, which means it's possible to repair it. In practice, a few cracks rarely justify the complete renewal of a ceiling; unless there are so many that the cost to repair them all, outweighs the cost of replacing the whole ceiling.

A different type of settlement is when timber joists get 'tired' from old age and sag under their own weight. Of course, the ceiling has no choice but to follow, causing a few extra cracks as the plasterwork tries to accommodate this extra stretching load. Sometimes sagging joists break away the plaster keys, ruining the plasterwork, but occasionally the lime mortar accommodates the movement and survives with only minor cracking. Such is the nature of relatively soft lime mortars when compared to modern materials, which are much less forgiving when stressed.

## MOVEMENT

You might think that movement is the same as settlement and you'd be partly right, but the distinction is that settlement is a result of specific 'one off' occurrences (a burst drain affecting the foundations for example). Whereas the movement I'm concerned with here is the natural day-to-day shifting of the house due to temperature change, humidity and live loads (you and your family!). In very old or poorly constructed ceilings, this regular movement may eventually crumble weak mortar keys, causing cracks and/ or sagging plasterwork.

Some types of movement are difficult to control (normal seasonal winter/ summer movement for example) and some houses have cracks that appear every year in the same place and at the same time. Put it down to the charm of living in an older house, it's just letting you know that it's still alive...

## WATER

Look for areas that are a different colour, usually darker but can be lighter too. Feel for actual damp areas or buy a cheap moisture meter and play around with it on your ceilings (or all over your house actually, you'll learn lots about the moisture levels in your home). In addition, when water dries out and evaporates all the dissolved salts and other minerals get left behind. So look out for white salty looking deposits, often in long wavy lines along joists, walls, ceilings etc. A digital 'laser' thermometer might be useful also, find the cold spots! Fun to play with too...

## SMALL WATER DAMAGE

This might be from a badly maintained roof (a slipped tile or wonky flashing etc.), a leaky appliance (dish washer, washing machine, fridge, etc.), or even a bad seal around the bathtub or shower tray (or a leaking door/ cubicle). Water gets into the ceiling little by little over time, eventually corroding nails, rotting timber and gradually causing the backing coat to deteriorate or crumble into its component parts, destroying the keys 'wraparound' connection to the laths.

## BIG WATER DAMAGE

These are obvious, 'one off' serious leaks. A damaged roof or a burst pipe usually. These flood the top of the ceiling and soak into the plaster, pooling on top until the weight is so great it finds a weak spot and starts to pour through the ceiling, often pulling the plasterwork down with it. Remember that a pint (½L) of water weighs a pound (½KG) and a leaking pipe or roof can spill hundreds of gallons (thousands of litres) if it occurs whilst you're at work for example (or worse, on holiday...).

Serious water damage to a lath and plaster ceiling is usually fairly catastrophic in nature and it's rare to be able to save one that's suffered a major or long-standing leak. Cutting out the damaged parts (or removing the whole ceiling) is often the only practical repair.

## LIVE LOADS

A live load is a polite term to describe little Johnny and his friends using the bed as a trampoline, jumping down onto the floor and rolling around!

All daily life in a house creates movement, which transmits small vibrations and shocks into the structure; even slamming doors (so no arguing okay?). Most of the time, the materials in your ceilings easily absorb this movement, but especially large shocks (like the now teenage Johnny playing football in his room with three of his burly friends) may be a little too much for the ceiling to cope with and damage will occur. Large shocks will flex the joists downwards, stretching the ceiling and damaging the plaster keys. Ongoing vibration and/or shocks will eventually break up the plasterwork around the keys/nibs until pieces start to fall down. Not good.

Treat your period home more like an elegant, aging Aunt rather than a twenty something party animal and your ceilings will thank you for your consideration. You need to be especially careful if the joists in your home are not quite as strong as they used to be, maybe due to age or even insect damage; the joists might even be a little undersized by today's standards, which leads nicely to...

## SUBSTANDARD WORK

I know, shocking huh? Nevertheless, poor quality or shoddy workmanship is not just a modern-day phenomenon. Folks often have the misguided idea that just because it's old, it has to be great quality. The reality can be far from that ideal. From housing built on a tight budget by cheap industrialists, to houses thrown up in a hurry after the war. Shoddy workmanship or poor material choice might mean your ceiling was not 100% perfect, even when it was new. Skimping on materials was commonplace in those leaner times; undersized joists, poorly graded joists (and often recycled joists or even upcycled ships spars...), not enough lime in the mortar; poor sand choices (dirty or badly graded) or even missing reinforcing horsehair. Any of the above usually leads to premature deterioration of the plasterwork on ceilings.

## HOW LATH AND PLASTER USUALLY FAILS

I know I keep banging on about 'keys' but honestly they really are a ....erm, 'key' component of your ceiling (sorry!). Over time and exacerbated by any damage mentioned above; keys crumble and break up. Without them, gravity grabs a hold of the heavy three coats of plaster and pulls it all south, just for the hell of it. Sometimes this means the plasterwork is literally just hanging underneath the laths by the horsehair strands in the mortar. Precarious? Little bit...

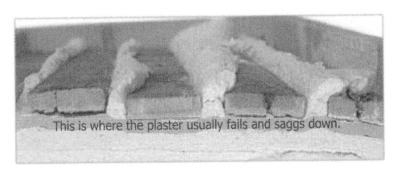

This is where the plaster usually fails and saggs down.

Once enough keys have broken, a ceiling becomes perilous (I love that word, perilous; we should drag it back into the mainstream...) and the plasterwork will separate from the laths completely and belly down. Eventually these bellies break up and the plasterwork falls to the floor, either in small pieces or in large sheets if there are aggravating factors (like a water leak or someone jumping on the floor above etc). Having said that, ceilings rarely fail over their entire area, some areas often remain perfectly fine even in ceilings that have started to fall down in places.

Occasionally damaged plaster keys are not the main culprit in the failure, sometimes the plaster coats themselves appear to 'delaminate', breaking up and falling away in sheets. This is usually due to workmanship issues such as...

- Poor control of moisture, i.e. including poor timing between plaster coats (too long/not long enough) or inappropriate conditions during the ceiling's installation (too hot/cold etc).

- Poor 'scratching' of base coats to provide a good key or grip for following coats.

- Using dirty or badly graded sands. Sand needs a proper mixture of sizes for best results. Too fine and it dries, shrinks and cracks, too coarse and the lime cannot fill the spaces, weakening it.

- Poor lime quality (or too little of it) lime needs to be mature and in the right quantity to coat each particle of sand to bind it all together.

## MAINTAIN AND REPAIR OR START OVER?

Don't panic just yet though. I know we've just gone through a whole list of worrying scenarios. However, please bear in mind that a damaged, cracked or sagging ceiling does not necessarily mean the plasterwork is irreparable. I'd be mortified if this guide leads to a single ceiling meeting an early and undignified demise because of a knee jerk reaction out of fear or ignorance.

Ideally of course, it would be nice to repair and maintain the original ceilings in our houses rather than rip them down and start over. However, that might not be practical (remember the new recessed lamps you want...) or even financially viable (your friendly neighbourhood plasterer promises you that it's much cheaper to rip it down and replace it with drywall). Ultimately the repair or replace question is down to how best to achieve the end result you want, plus whether you are doing the work yourself or hiring in plasterers (and of course, the resulting cost).

When you look at costs, it's often about percentages. Once more than half of a ceiling has failed, total replacement may be a cheaper option than repairs. Check the entire ceiling as described earlier and mark any areas you think have separated with big pencil circles. From the floor try to judge how much of the ceiling has failed by visually/ mentally 'adding up' all your pencil marks.

If circumstances do dictate the ceiling has to go, the second, lesser decision is deciding on a replacement. Whether to go traditional and replace it using like for like materials (appropriate, authentic but more time consuming and thus costlier) or whether to use modern materials like drywall (quicker, easier and cheaper).

It's inevitable that drywall looks an attractive option for those wanting to 'DIY' a new ceiling themselves and I can't deny that it's great material to work with and will give you easy to install, flat ceilings. You'll know if you want to go the traditional route and let's leave it at that. It's not fair to criticise anyone who decides to replace a traditional ceiling with drywall, each to their own and all that.

When it comes to DIY or hiring in, it's all about the skills you have and what you're prepared to learn. It's true that many DIY folks are scared to tackle 'wet work' like traditionally plastering a ceiling with lime mortar or even just 'skimming' drywall with modern plaster. But don't be deterred, see the resources section at the end of the book for some really good guides/videos to re-plastering with lime products. It's not as difficult as you'd think, especially if you build a practice panel and try a few times before-hand or you could take a short 'homeowners' plastering course. Lime is perfect for budding handy folks because it's forgiving and slow; very slow setting when compared to modern 'all done in a couple of hours' materials. And imagine the sense of achievement!

However, if you are going to go traditional and want to hire someone in, further problems arise if local tradespeople are not very familiar with using lime products (even though the skills required are broadly the same as used for cement-based products). You might need to go further afield to find a specialist and of course, anything 'specialist' pushes the cost up. You could try reading up yourself and then convince/educate your builder/plasterer to 'have a go' with lime products, (it's how I was converted many years ago!). Trust me, if you can plaster with a cement-based mortar, then you can plaster with lime mortar, no worries. Hiring in for drywall is no problem, everyone and their dog is familiar with it, and it's very easy to get a very good finish.

One last option to consider; I've even seen lots of ceilings (and walls) replaced with lightweight wooden or MDF panelling, both of which are good options for anyone who wants to DIY but is terrified by the 'wet stuff'; or maybe I've just been in Norway too long, (wooden panelling is v. common here!).

Right then, assuming you're going to keep your ceiling, lets go through the options you have to keep it going for a few more years... (you can skip the next chapter if you've already decided to remove yours)...

# 7 WAYS TO REPAIR YOUR CEILING

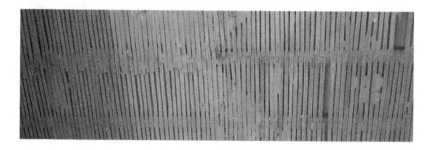

OK, so you've decided to give your lath and plaster ceiling a little 'lurve' hmm? Well, most people agree that traditional lath and plaster really adds charm and enhances the feeling of living in a period house, so it's definitely a smart thing to do. The good news is, that it's often possible to repair lath and plaster ceilings (or walls for that matter) and get years more life out of them.

What route you choose depends on...

- The existing state of the ceiling.

- The look or feel you're aiming for.

- Your budget (or daddy's generosity...).

- Your 'tolerance' of erm.....how can I put it; 'rustic' looking surfaces!

It's a universal truth that the 'flatter' and most 'long lived' repairs cost more to carry out, plus the older your lath and plaster is, the more work it's likely to need.

My work on period homes has brought me into contact with all sorts of interesting people. Some folks that revel in the old-world charm of a place, forgiving it all manner of sins in pursuit of the country house lifestyle. But I've also seen folks with minimalistic urges who like everything flawless. Every kind of finish is possible with lath and plaster.... given enough time, oh and enough money of course.

Pretty much in order of cost/ complexity/ longevity, let's get started and have a look at seven ways you can improve a reasonable lath and plaster ceiling that you want to keep for a little while longer...

## 1: RE-DECORATE AS IT IS

I know, I know, this hardly need saying, but we have to start the list somewhere and this simple solution is sometimes suitable for those who love authenticity, warts and all. It's also only suitable for ceilings that are structurally sound, if a little crazed and worn. Arguably too, this is not even a repair but basic maintenance.

You'll need to find out what type of paint is already on the ceiling, and for the best results simply follow up with more of the same. Your local professional paint store will be your best friend here for help and advice (don't worry they're asked stuff like this all the time). Especially seek advice on paint if you think you might be switching 'sides'. i.e. changing the type of paint (from limewash to latex/emulsion for example). Some paint types don't play well with others and adverse reactions can occur, creating a lot of extra work to put right.

## COST

- Very, very economical 'repair', (especially if you paint with limewash, which is the cheapest finish around).

## PROS

- Quick to carry out.

- Minimum amount of mess.

- Period charm in abundance.

- Ideal for very old cottages that don't have a straight edge or surface in them.

- Good way to tidy up a ceiling which is on your mid to long term maintenance plan.

- Doesn't remove any of the 'historic' fabric of the building and arguably maintains it a little.

- Shows imperfections, and I mean all of them...

## CONS

- Not a serious 'repair' and especially if the plasterwork has gone beyond the hairline cracking stage, i.e. any sagging areas, bigger cracks or missing plaster.

- Potentially dangerous option if the ceiling is in a very poor condition.

- Hides nothing and it's not likely to be a 'flat' or modern looking finish.

●)━• Shows imperfections!

**HOW**

●)━• Vacuum all dust away.

●)━• Gently wash down the whole ceiling if required using sugar/ decorators' soap and a sponge (especially if dirty and always, always over dubious looking stains like tobacco or water).

●)━• Apply a stain block over any stains that might 'bleed' through (and always for tobacco, old water stains etc).

●)━• Re-decorate following the directions on the tin. Preferably with a lime-based paint (if the ceiling is completely original) or most likely with suitable breathable water-based paint. Paint into the hairline cracks to seal them, (but remember paint isn't a filler) and keep a 'backward' eye open for drips/ runs for a lot longer than you'd think possible (i.e. go back and check a few times).

## 2: REPAIR THE CRACKS

If the plasterwork has minor cracking or is crazed but still firmly adhered around the laths, you can fill the cracks/ blemishes and redecorate. It's important to find a good decorator's filler here. Get one that is smooth and creamy, which makes it easy to press into small cracks and level off. Because no one in their right mind likes sanding right? Oh and make sure the filler is easily sandable too... you know, just in case.

NOTE: Some 'ready to use' fillers are harder to work with than a 'powder' type; they seem to be coarser and have more 'body' (if you follow me). It only takes a few seconds to mix up powdered filler with water in an empty plastic container (i.e. not your lunch box...) and then you can have it whatever consistency you like to work with, super smooth being my preference, (about like tooth-paste).

Also, remember it's best to fill in cracks and carry out caulking in advance of the anticipated decorating date, despite what it says on the 'tube' etc. Caulk may be 'ready' for painting after one hour, but I assure you, it'll be even *more ready* the next day...

## COST

- Economical repair. Fillers and caulks are cheap, and only a couple of cheap tools are required.

## PROS

- Retains the period feel of the ceiling.

- Looks very good, at least initially.

- Easy and quick repair.

- Very little mess.

- Doesn't remove the 'historic' fabric of the building.

## CONS

- Might only look good for a few years depending on the plasterwork's original structural integrity.

- Not suitable for medium to badly damaged ceilings.

## HOW

- Lightly scrape out the cracks and vacuum out any loose material (using a brush attachment is best).

- Small or hairline cracks benefit from a little deepening and widening out (a slim V shape is good) using the edge of your scraper. This gives the filler somewhere to go and avoids the plaster building up over the hairline crack causing ridges.

- Wash down the whole ceiling if required (and always if there are tobacco or water stains).

- Prime the cracks with a suitable plaster primer, or some slightly thinned water-based paint. At the very least dampen the cracks with a little water, because essentially, they are a 'new', bare plaster surface and will suck the 'life' out of your filler and possibly shrink (losing its grip on the sides of the cracks...).

- Fill cracks and small blemishes with decorators' filler using a suitably sized scraper or small drywall spreader. Push in the filler with the scraper at 90 degrees to the crack, press to flatten out and scrape off excess by running the scraper along the crack. Repeat as necessary until the crack is full with no dips. Hold the scraper/filler tool at a shallow angle to the ceiling and run it along the filler for a final smoothing. This should leave it needing little (if any) sanding.

- After a few hours, repeat the above step to fill in any areas where the filler has shrunk back a little. On deeper parts, more layers may be necessary (I know, shocking huh! Filler shrinks, learn to live with it and do it again... and again!).

- Once the filler is dry, gently sand the filled areas flat using 120 grit paper. If you're careful and methodical with the fill-ing tool, you shouldn't need more than a light scuff with 120grit sand paper just to remove any nibs, lines etc. at the edges. If you want really top-quality results, a light finish sanding with a 150-180 grit sandpaper works well.

- Vacuum all dust away or gently brush the ceiling with a very soft sweeping brush or a big feather duster like I do (but don't tell anyone, I love my feather duster!).

- Re-decorate following the directions on the tin. Preferably with a lime-based paint (if the ceiling is completely original) or most likely with suitable breathable water-based paint (double check with the guy in the store).

NOTE: It's also possible to fill fine cracks with a flexible decorator's caulk. Run along the crack using caulk gun with the nozzle tight over the crack, press in further using a flexible scraper working across the crack, removing any excess by dampening the flexible scraper and running along the crack. Some folks finish off with a well wrung out fine celled sponge as a final flourish (don't use the same sponge you use on the car though!). And remember that can't sandpaper caulk.

## 3: USE A THICK LINING PAPER

You can greatly improve a relatively sound lath and plaster ceilings appearance and stability using a good quality, thick lining paper. Lining paper has the benefit of 'tightening' everything up and giving the ceiling a uniform look without necessarily spoiling the aged feel of the ceiling. Lining paper shrinks back into every part of the ceiling, so it won't hide the worst of the contours (so fill and sand them first for best results), but it does give a ~~cracking~~ (oops!) brilliant surface to decorate. Ironically, I've seen plenty painted to look 'distressed'... go figure.

**COST**

➤ Economical repair.

**PROS**

➤ Retains that sought-after period feel.

➤ Creates a great surface for decorating on.

➤ Gains many more years out of reasonable plasterwork.

➤ Doesn't remove the 'historic' fabric of the building.

**CONS**

➤ Relatively difficult to wallpaper overhead/ on uneven surfaces, especially if you're not used to papering.

➤ Doesn't hide everything, lining paper is not a 'cure all' and it won't make your surfaces perfect.

➤ Won't stop further cracking over time if the plasterwork is deteriorating or moving around.

**HOW**

➤ Lining paper will highlight any cracks by shrinking into them as it dries. If a superior finish is required, follow the steps outlined in repair 2 ("Repair the Cracks") to fill any cracks or small defects first, (minus the final decorating) before 'hanging' the lining paper.

➤ Once the ceiling is dry after washing/filling etc. apply a thick lining paper to the whole ceiling, cutting in carefully at the edges (unless you're fitting cornice afterwards).

- Lining paper comes in different 'grades', ranging from 800 to 2000 (in the UK). You might only find the lighter grades in DIY stores, so you'll need to head into a specialist decorators trade store for thicker grades (or online of course).

- Generally, the worse the ceiling, the thicker the paper you should use for the best (read flattest) results. 1000 grade is considered 'standard' but 1200 or 1400 gives better results on old ceilings, with the very thickest grade reserved for rough ceilings. Higher grades of lining paper are slightly less pliable (than the thinner ones) and need a little more skill to hang.

- Re-decorate your new 'blank canvas' as you wish, water-based paint usually, but sometimes folks choose wallpaper (I know, that seems a bit odd, right?).

## 4: PLASTER/ SKIM/ VENEER THE WHOLE CEILING

Hmm... controversial one here, and I don't personally recommend it, although I was 'guilty' in my earlier years (30 years ago!). However, I'll include it here because it's still a very popular option recommended by many well-meaning plasterers and some folks jump on it like fresh buns because it's a 'quick fix' when compared to removal.

The idea is to completely 're-skim' finely crazed and tired old plasterwork with two thin coats of modern gypsum-based finish plaster, ending up around 3 to 5mm (1/8th to 3/16th) thick overall, (a thin 'veneer' if you like).

One idea involves incorporating a layer or sheet of fine glass-fibre mesh (like a wider version of drywall joint mesh), which is trowelled into the first coat of plaster. However this mesh is expensive and often needs to be specially ordered at many smaller builders' supply stores.

Whilst this method can tighten up the plasterwork on an old ceiling and look great initially, due to the relative stiffness of the new plaster (in comparison to the underlying lath and plaster-work), it might develop cracks later; or not. It really depends on how stable the ceiling is to begin with (very difficult to quantify accurately). Sorry to be so pessimistic, but I'm just telling you how it is!

**COST**

⊃)– Medium cost repair.

**PROS**

⊃)– Relatively quick repair when compared to replacing the whole ceiling.

⊃)– Less mess than total replacement.

⊃)– Doesn't remove the 'historic' fabric of the building.

⊃)– Creates a good surface for decorating on.

**CONS**

⊃)– Potential for the harder, modern plaster to crack as the softer lime-based plaster underneath continues to move with the house.

- Potential for the new plaster to 'de-laminate' and fall away, if the old plasterwork is not clean and well prepared for the new plaster.

**HOW**

Not sure why I'm writing this, as I don't recommend it! So, again one last time, this method should only be considered as a last resort as it's considered poor practice.

But if you insist...

- Scrape all loose material from the ceiling and deepen/ scrape out any cracks.

- Wash the ceiling with sugar soap or other suitable pre- paint cleaner and allow to dry.

- Prime the ceiling with a sealer/primer following the instructions on the tin. Usually one coat is applied and allowed to dry, followed by a second coat shortly before plastering.

- On top of the dry primer (but before the second coat if applicable) apply a self-adhesive joint tape over any cracks. OR: apply mesh to whole ceiling (see next).

- If available and applicable, bed a thin fiberglass mesh into the first coat of plaster. Cut these to size before starting so that they are ready.

- Plaster as normal. Usually two thin coats applied 'wet on wet' and trowelled up as it starts to harden. Finish thickness usually 3 to 5mm depending on conditions and flatness of the ceiling.

# 5: REPAIR LOOSE OR MISSING PLASTER

If most of the ceiling is sound, but there are some small areas of missing or loose plasterwork, you can re-plaster the damaged areas and then follow the advice in repair 2: ("Repair the Cracks") to finish off any smaller cracks on the rest of the ceiling before decorating. This is a good method for localised damage after a specific event like a water leak. It'd be a shame to tear down the whole ceiling just because of damage to a small part of it. Think of it like repairing a car to keep it going. After all, you'd not buy a new car just because you dinged the door, would you?

Repairing the ceiling using 'like for like' traditional materials is of course the most authentic way to go; but in my opinion, if faced with little practical alternative, small repairs using modern lightweight materials is preferable to taking down the whole ceiling and replacing with drywall.

## COST

- Medium cost repair depending how large an area needs replacing/ re-plastering.

## PROS

- Largely retains the period feel.

- Relatively quick repair when compared to replacing the whole ceiling.

- Less mess than total replacement.

- Doesn't remove the 'historic' fabric of the building.

## CONS

- Needs reasonable DIY Skills, many find applying wet materials difficult to master. Practice is usually required to build a little experience, especially since it will be overhead on a ceiling.

- Modern plasters (if used) might be too 'rigid' alongside your old plaster leading to some cracking where the two different materials meet.

- Depending on what caused the damage to the ceiling in the first place, other areas that appear sound now may start to fail in the future. Therefore, this repair might only last a few years before you need to carry out further work.

## HOW

- It's recommended to carry out repairs using similar haired lime-based mortars and plasters used on the original ceiling. It's not as hard as it first appears. See No.5 in the chapter '5 Ways to Replace your Ceiling' for more details.

- If traditional materials are not an option for you, then areas could (in theory) be re-plastered using modern lightweight backing plasters and finish plaster (non-protected ceilings only).

- Your local builder's merchant will have some good suggestions for suitable lightweight, modern plasters if you tell them what you are doing.

- Remove any loose plaster/ dust before re-plastering.

- Ensure the gaps between any visible laths are clear to allow plaster to go through and provide a good key. Replace any damaged or missing lath with new ones or cover the gaps with a plasterer's expanded metal mesh lathing (google it!).

- I have seen damaged areas of lath and plaster repaired using drywall several times. Cut out the damaged lath and plaster in square sections back to the joists. Screw tile lath (or similar) to the sides of the joists 19mm to 24mm (¾" to 1") up from the finished ceiling level. Screw up new drywall. Apply one or two layers of lightweight backing plaster suitable for drywall and finally with a two-coat finish plaster (skimming in UK).

A second method is to leave the old laths in place and stick drywall up almost flush with the surrounding plaster using drywall board adhesive. 'Skim' to finish.

See note two in the 'cons' above related to these methods though, it's a compromise...

- Damp down any dry areas a little before re-plastering (or use a suitable plaster primer), especially the old edges of the surrounding plasterwork which will be bone dry and suck out all the moisture from the new materials causing them to curl away and crack.

- Vacuum all dust away.

- Wash down the non-repaired sections of the ceiling if required.

- Re-decorate following the directions on the tin. Preferably with a lime-based paint (if the ceiling is completely original) or most likely with suitable breathable water based paint.

## 6: USE A GLUE 'SYSTEM' TO FIX SAGGING

Sagging plasterwork can (in theory at least) be 'glued' back into place. Usually done by...

- Drilling many holes through the damaged areas of plaster-work, stopping at the lath.

- Carefully vacuuming out the dust.

- Injecting a suitable tube type adhesive.

- Gently pushing the plasterwork back into place.

- Supporting it until the adhesive dries.

- Patch filling the holes and cracks afterwards.

It's a fair repair and although on a bad ceiling you might be looking at hundreds of holes, each hole only takes a few seconds to do.

Years ago this type of repair never occurred to us and we routinely removed damaged ceilings with nary a thought to preserving the houses originality. Nowadays folks are much more aware and sensitive to such things and so in recent years new methods of preserving these old ceilings have emerged. Although primarily used to 'fix' cracks, it's fine to repair smaller dropped areas of sagging plasterwork like this. The upshot is that it doesn't cost much to experiment with this method. Grab a tube of soft adhesive and a couple of those cheap 'telescopic quick props' or a few lengths of 'tile laths' and you're in business. If the experiment doesn't work very well for your ceiling, well, you're only back where you started. Going gently and methodically is paramount, oh and you'll need a good amount of patience...

There is even a 'system' available in the USA called "Big Wally's Plaster Magic" just google it and watch the video to learn more about this method of repair. The guys at 'Old House Online' also have a great article that explains how to glue up a sagging ceiling perfectly, you can find it here...

www.oldhouseonline.com/how-to-fix-plaster-ceilings/

## COST

- Medium cost, depending on time taken and plasterwork condition, (i.e. how many holes need working on and over what area).

- Don't forget to add in the cost of finishing the ceiling (filling any cracks etc.) See earlier in this chapter.

- Retains period feel and looks.

- Not too difficult as a DIY proposition (see cons!).

- Doesn't remove the 'historic' fabric of the building.

## CONS

- Medium term effectiveness (although long term is quite possible, depending on the ceiling).

- Arguably, some say it's a specialised job and it's true, it may be too fiddly for some DIY repairers due to the patience required. You'll also need a 'nose' for how much is enough, when it comes to handling/ pushing up old plasterwork.

- Relatively new method, but it's difficult to see how it can make things worse...

## HOW

- Drill 5mm (3/16") or so holes through the plaster, stopping at the lath. Drill another hole nearby if you hit the gap in between the laths (it happens about 15% of the time!).

- Gently vacuum the dust out of the hole, bracing the nozzle against the ceilings with your fingers.

(Some adhesives benefit from damping down behind the holes slightly using a pump spray, you'll need to check the directions on the adhesives locally available to you.)

- Damp the hole down with a sprayer (if applicable for your adhesive). Hold it tight up to the hole so that the fine spray goes into and damps down the lath and plaster above, (I push short lengths of rubber hose over the nozzles which stops the water going everywhere and running down your sleeve...). Some folks even include a little plaster sealer into the pump spray but if you do, you'll need to clean out the sprayer each day.

- Push the nozzle of the adhesive gently into the hole and give it a couple of pumps or 'squirts'. A thin water friendly solvent free adhesive is best.

- Glue up several holes in one go; as many as you can do in a few minutes, depending on the 'open' time stated on your adhesive's directions.

- Very gently push up and support the area you've just glued up using blanket-covered pieces of timber or plywood, gently wedged up to the ceiling with tile laths. If you intend to do a lot of this kind of work, instead of blankets, staple strips of old carpet (furry side up) onto your wood and get some telescopic quick props, which are a great pair of 'second hands'.

- Some folks back this up or replace this step by inserting drywall screws into the holes but you'll need to be careful not to create 'elephants' footprints across the ceiling... Slightly countersink the holes too, using a handheld countersink tool.

- Remove supports once the glue has dried and scrape off any glue residue; fill the holes or small cracks and then sand down.

- Vacuum all dust away.

- Wash down the ceiling if required.

- Re-decorate following the directions on the tin. Preferably with a lime based paint (if the ceiling is completely original) or most likely with suitable breathable water based paint.

NOTE: An alternative method is to drill the holes from above through the lath (but it's much trickier to stop the drill before it goes through the plaster!).

## 7:  PRESERVE A 'PROTECTED' CEILING

Given enough time and money, you can repair and rescue even the worst ceilings; but to be honest, this kind of investment is usually restricted to historically valuable ceilings in order to satisfy local conservation authorities.

**COST**

- Expensive due to the amount of extreme care needed and labour involved.

**PROS**

- Retains all original period features.

- Preserves historically valuable plasterworks for future generations to enjoy.

**CONS**

- Relatively complicated, expensive, and could necessitate the need to hire a specialist contractor rather than your average high street builder.

- Arguably a difficult DIY prospect (but by no means impossible).

- Time consuming (very).

**HOW**

Arguably, beyond the scope of this brief guide, but to give you an idea what's involved...

- Fully support sagging plasterwork from underneath on blanket covered timber on props or staging.

- Working from above, gently remove all the accumulated dust, debris and loose keys or nibs that are sitting on top of the ceiling.

- Gently push the fully supported plasterwork back up to the laths.

- Stabilise the plasterwork using bonding agents or acrylic adhesives, (it's often weak and crumbly).

- Re-attach the plasterwork to the laths using an approved repair procedure approved and recommended by your local authority's conservation officer.

NOTES: After stabilising the plasterwork using special chemicals, a typical method to reattach the plasterwork to the laths is to fix a wire mesh tray to the inside edges of the joists, just above the plasterwork, and then apply adhesive to the stabilized plasterwork embedding the mesh, effectively reattaching the plasterwork to the lath.

Alternatively, and gaining more favour nowadays is to support the ceiling from below using stainless steel washers and fasteners set into shallow cut-outs in the plaster and patched up afterwards (similar to the "Big Wally's Plaster Magic" system talked about in repair 5 earlier). Less weight on the laths and more effective.

- At this level, you'll no doubt be told how to finish off your ceiling by the local conservation officer, otherwise re-decorate following the directions on the tin with a suitable product, compatible with the ceilings existing finish.

**CEILING TOO BAD FOR REPAIRS?**

If none of the above methods of repair sound like they'll give you the ceilings you want, then the next step is to replace it with something else... read on.

# 5 WAYS TO REPLACE YOUR CEILING

I n other words, what to do when you realise your existing lath and plaster won't give you what you want or because it's deteriorated too far to save. This list is pretty much in order of cost and complexity. Here are some options to consider after your poor old ceiling hits the floor in a cloud of dust...

## 1: REMOVE EXISTING AND EXPOSE THE JOISTS

I know, I know, this hardly qualifies as 'replacing' now does it? But still, leaving the beams exposed is super popular in older cottages where the timbers are irregular, or hand cut as they add lots of character and period charm. But nowadays, exposing the joists is not just restricted to cottages and you'll see it in lots of different house styles.

Basically, you'd remove every scrap of lath and plaster and clean up all the timberwork. But don't forget that this timberwork was never supposed to see the light of day, so don't underestimate the time it takes to get the timbers etc. to look good. Then you can carry out any additional work to wiring and pipework. It's popular to install false ceilings in between the joists, conveniently hiding any new services you want, like cables for new lamps or a water pipe for that new ice-making fridge...

## COST

- Economical to medium depending on the timberworks condition.

## PROS

- Easy DIY solution as little skill needed.

- Easy to build service runs by adding 'false' ceilings, high up in between the joists.

- Charming, period, 'old cottage' look or retro depending on the finishes used.

- Creates the feeling of a higher ceiling (especially if painted with lighter colours).

## CONS

- Different look and feel, arguably only suited to certain properties and owners.

- Slightly limited choice of light fittings due to lack of a flat, conventional ceiling. Small spotlights, fitted to the side of the joists are common.

- Can look awkward if joists are not spaced properly or if the room includes areas trimmed out, such as around chimneys.

- Loss of the original 'historic' fabric of the building.

## HOW

- Completely remove the lath and plaster as described in the next chapter 'Removing Lath and Plaster'.

- Wire brush, sandpaper or scrape all plaster marks off the timberwork. Be careful if using a machine (like a wire brush on a drill or a sander) as it's easy to snag up on remnants of old nails etc.

- Repair any damage or holes in the timberwork using a suitable stainable/paintable wood filler or cut in new pieces of timber etc.

- Create damage! The newly exposed joists may be too square and uniform for you. Roughen up, dent and gouge the timber, using tools (cold chisel, hammer, bars, length of chain etc.) to create the effect you like, especially on the corners.

- Re-route existing and add new runs of wiring or pipes, as applicable. Alternatively, if it's not possible to re-route, hide them instead. One way to hide services is to fit strips of drywall in between the joists on small battens nailed or screwed onto the side of the joists providing a 'duct' under-

neath the floorboards above. This often looks better propor-
tionally and effectively hides the underside of the floorboards above.

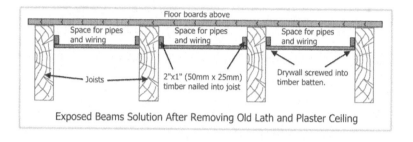

Exposed Beams Solution After Removing Old Lath and Plaster Ceiling

✄→ Clean up and vacuum all surfaces. Leave as is or decorate
with varnish, wood stain, or paint.

## 2: OVERBOARD WITH DRYWALL

Probably one of the most popular solutions is to cover up a
lath and plaster ceiling by 'over-boarding' with drywall, using
long drywall screws through the existing lath and plaster and into
the joists. Arguably, this is not an ideal solution (see cons below),
but you'll hear this option discussed as though it's the 'only' option
by many. Obviously, in occupied houses it avoids the horrible
mess created by complete removal.

New wiring and pipe runs are installed by breaking small
holes in the lath and plaster at intervals and pulling (called fish-
ing) cables and pipes into the space above the ceiling. The new
drywall covers up the holes.

**COST**

➣— Medium to high.

**PROS**

➣— Effectively a new drywall surface is created, ready for decorating how you wish.

➣— Minimises mess by retaining the existing ceiling.

➣— Doesn't remove the 'historic' fabric of the building (technically at least).

**CONS**

➣— Loses that period feel.

➣— Potential problem as the existing plaster may continue to come away from the laths and end up sitting on top of the new drywall, stressing the fasteners.

➣— Potential problems with levels if there is a cornice.

➣— The screws will try to pull the flat drywall board into the ceiling's curves, dips and bumps etc. This usually leads them to tear through the paper, weakening their hold and could mean 'popped heads' in the future.

**HOW**

NOTE: This 'how' section covers the steps peculiar to "overboarding"; read this in conjunction with the chapter *Installing Drywall* to finish off the explanation.

➣— Find the direction of the joists by assuming that they are the opposite way to the floorboards above (or look in the attic.).

➤❯╾ Repeat the work in the following paragraph "Finding Joists" all around the edge of the room to find each joist. Start close to the wall where you suspect there might be joists. (Ignore anyone who tells you to screw drywall up anywhere, relying on the laths... although, if it's really unavoidable you might get away with small overhangs at the edges....).

**FINDING JOISTS**

The quickest (if not cleanest) way to find joists is to drill a line of holes 38mm (1½") apart where you suspect there are joists. You will feel the resistance when you hit the joist (in comparison to drilling straight through the lath and plaster. When you find a joist, drill more holes to find each side of the joist. Mark each side well. Be very aware that you are drilling 'blind', be careful to only just drill through the lath and plaster in case there are wires or worse, water pipes just above (not terribly likely right on top of the L&P but not impossible...). Now you know how wide the joist is and where it is. Guestimate where you're likely to find the next joist (based on them most likely being 400mm to 600mm (16" to 24") apart). Repeat along both sides of the room.

NOTE: Some folks report some success using joist or stud finders on lath and plaster, but my experience has been patchy. I think this is due to the varying density common in lath and plaster ceilings which confuses the readings.

➤❯╾ Put a temporary nail in the middle of your marks to denote the centre of a joist. Hold up a chalk line, wall to wall, touching both nails. Flick the chalk line to mark the ceiling and then extend the chalk line down both walls (at least 1" (25m) using a pencil so you can see the marks once you are holding a drywall board in place. This centre line denotes where to put your drywall screws. Remove temporary nails.

- Re-route existing or run your new cables and pipes as applicable.

- If the room is going to be a kitchen or a bathroom, consider installing a vapour barrier. Staple a thin polythene layer over the whole ceiling first (or use a foil backed drywall board). Bedrooms/ other living rooms are usually fine without.

- Now you're ready to over-board with drywall using long drywall screws, through the old L & P into the joists where you have marked. Usually 60mm to 75mm (2 1/2" to 3") screws to ensure the screw goes in an absolute minimum of 25mm (1") into good solid timber.

- Be prepared to cut the ends of the drywall to ensure the end joints centre over a joist. Some folks rely on screwing the board ends into the lath and plaster alone wherever they fall, creating 'flying joints', but it's bad practice IMHO.

- Finish off the drywall as normal (see 'Installing Drywall' chapter).

- Re-decorate your blank canvas as you wish, water-based paint or even wallpaper.

## 3: BATTEN OUT AND INSTALL DRYWALL

A better alternative to straightforward over-boarding with drywall is to add small timber battens first. This is an especially good repair as the battens secure the old plasterwork preventing it from falling down, (ever) and the new drywall gives you an 'as new' finish. In addition, the batten thickness creates a convenient duct that's perfect for new cable runs for new lighting or pipes for new fixtures etc. You also have the option to add insulation into this space if that's a useful added benefit for you.

The other big plus for this method is the opportunity to level up or flatten old saggy ceilings by inserting shims underneath the battens as they go up, working out from the lowest point, (see the chapter 'Levelling Up Joists').

## COST

- Medium to high, depending whether you level up the ceiling at the same time.

## PROS

- A new drywall surface is created, ready for decorating how you wish.

- Minimises the mess as there's no need to remove the existing ceiling.

- Doesn't remove the 'historic' fabric of the building (in theory at least).

- Permanently secures the old damaged ceiling.

- Creates an easy duct for new services.

- Possibility to flatten or level up sagging ceilings using shims under the battens.

- A permanent repair.

**CONS**

- Loss of ceiling height.

- Conflict of levels if there is a cornice or if the windows are full height and go up to the ceiling.

- Potential problem of adding weight to poor joists, although arguably if they are poor, replace them!

**HOW**

- Check the ceiling for flatness and/or level (if important to you) using a large straight edge, spirit level or taut string line.

- Determine if you are happy to let the battens 'go with the flow' over the existing ceilings gentle bumps and hollows or whether you want to create a perfectly flat or level ceiling by shimming or packing the battens until they are level/ flat.

- If you want to level up the ceiling, see the 'Cross Battens' section in the chapter 'Levelling Up Joists'.

- Screw appx 25mm x 50mm (1" x 2") battens, long side up, underneath the existing lath and plasterwork, by screwing through it and into the existing ceiling joists. You can go either way with the battens; along the underside of the joists (better supports the old plasterwork) or across or 90 degrees to the joists (If it's better for your piping or wiring etc).

NOTE: Screws must penetrate good, solid wood in the joist by around 38mm (1 ½") or more.

- After fastening up the battens, re-route existing, or run new cables and pipes as applicable, clipping them to the side of the battens or into the laths above.

- Small gaps can be left out of the battens (in between where the drywall screws will go) if you need to run services both ways on the ceiling, but you must be very careful when screwing up the drywall not to hit them as you'll likely hit the services underneath.

- Lastly, install drywall as normal (see the later chapter 'Installing Drywall').

- Re-decorate your blank canvas as you wish, water based paint or even wallpaper.

## 4: REMOVE EXISTING AND INSTALL DRYWALL

You need to pull information from several chapters to do this... First, completely remove the ceiling as described in the chapter 'Removing Lath and Plaster'. If you need to level up the ceiling joists (not terribly likely, but in an older house, maybe...) follow the description in the chapter 'Levelling Up Ceilings'. Then run your new services (if required) and to finish, install new drywall as described in the chapter 'Installing Drywall'.

### COST

- High cost. Complete removal of the old ceiling material plus the installation of new drywall and finishing makes this one of the most expensive options.

**PROS**

- New drywall ceiling, stable and very flat.

- Easy to run new services.

- Removes the original damaged/unsafe ceiling.

- A permanent repair.

**CONS**

- Loses the period feel.

- Loss of the original fabric of the building.

**HOW**

- Remove the existing lath and plaster and de-nail all joists (see 'Removing Lath and Plaster').

- Re-route existing or run your new cables and pipes as applicable.

- Check joists/ceiling for level (if applicable) and correct any discrepancies (see 'Levelling Up Ceilings).

- Install drywall as normal (see 'Installing Drywall').

- Re-decorate your blank canvas as you wish, water-based paint or even wallpaper.

# 5: TRADITIONAL RE-PLASTER WITH LIME

Arguably, this is the benchmark solution, the 'proper' way to replace an old lath and plaster ceiling damaged beyond repair. It's authentic and appropriate. It's also time consuming and requires some skill and experience. This makes it expensive to hire in folks to do it for you, as these days it's a 'specialist' job. However, in my humble opinion, it's by no means impossible to learn with a little practice and patience, especially if you've done 'wet work' before using cement mortar or modern plaster.

Essentially the old ceiling is completely removed and replaced with like for like traditional materials, very similar to the original ceiling. Usually this means nailing up new laths and re-plastering with a suitable two-coat haired lime mortar, followed by a two very thin coats of a lime finish coat plaster.

Because of the ease and cheapness of using drywall as a re-placement, traditional materials are (sadly) often only considered on houses of historical significance. However, not only is it en-tirely possible to replace any traditionally built ceiling with like for like materials, it is both correct and admirable to do so. Even if you think yours is 'only' a 'modest' home. Arguably, using harder modern products in a traditionally built house causes long-term damage as well as robbing it of its proper character (check out the Resources section at the end of the book for some really good guides to re-plastering with lime products, it's not as difficult as you'd think).

## COST

- High if hiring in, due to 'special' skills and the comparatively longer time needed. Materials may also cost a little more than equivalent drywall products.

## PROS

- Good as new finish that matches the surrounding period plasterwork.

- This repair will age appropriately and is able to move and breathe with the rest of the building.

- Earns lots of 'kudos' from all involved and all who see your magnificent new lath and plaster ceiling! Enjoy the self-satisfied feeling of a job well done.

- Long-term repair.

**CONS**

- Possibly a difficult DIY proposition for some because of the need to learn some 'wet plasterwork' skills.

- Often difficult to find tradesmen willing to work with traditional materials like lime mortars and plasters (although there's no valid reason for this).

- Time consuming as traditional materials can take a long time to dry out between coats.

- Difficult to carry out lime plasterwork in the wintertime unless heating is in place.

**HOW**

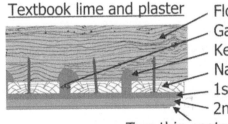

Textbook lime and plaster

- Floor or ceiling joist
- Gap between laths
- Keys or nibs of plaster
- Nailed lath
- 1st coat lime plaster
- 2nd coat lime plaster

Two thin coats of lime finish plaster

Let's start with a quick look at how your ceiling is constructed. The previous image shows how a textbook ceiling will look if we cut through it and look at its cross section...

Many of the trowel skills for traditional materials are *very* similar to those used to work with any wet material (cement-based mortars, gypsum plasters etc.). In other words, if you can work with cement mortar, you'll be fine with lime mortar.

In fact, I believe lime mortar is especially good for beginners because it sets so slowly, and the mortar can be endlessly re-mixed. This removes the time pressure to get finished prevalent with cement mortars and modern plaster. When I bought my first 25KG tub of lime putty I naively asked, "how long will it last" (still thinking in modern plaster terms) and the guy, said "Hmm, well, I'd say about, Oh a hundred years or so... probably longer"!

Premixed mortars last a long time and, in many cases, the older the lime putty is to make it, the better the material is. Just don't store it once you've added in the hair reinforcement, mix up only what you need each day.

## THE BASIC PROCEDURE...

- Nail thin pieces of lath to the underside of the joists aiming for gaps not less than 6mm (¼") and ideally around 10mm (3/8"). Always use rust proof lath nails and get copper, zinc or stainless steel for oak because of the stronger natural acids present.

- Don't forget to leave a gap next to the wall with the first lath.

- If your joists are wider than 50mm (2") you'll need to nail a 'counter lath' on the underside of the joists first. This allows the plaster to wrap around the ceiling laths underneath the joist itself (imagine a 100mm (4") wide joist where the plaster goes into the gap between the laths but then stops at the underside of a joist that's going to be flexing up and down slightly... A counter lath allows keys under the joist.

## SUCTION CONTROL AND BONDING

- Start damping down the laths and any dry plasterworks at the edges the day before plastering. Repeat again an hour or so before plastering. This stops the old materials pulling excess moisture out of the new mortar causing it to shrink excessively as it dries out.

- Use a garden sprayer set to a fine mist. Many light sprays are better than heavy soakings, which will simply drip onto the floor.

- Alternatively, some folks like to use a plaster primer to seal all those dry and porous areas.

## APPLYING THE PLASTER

- Knock up your (previously mixed) batch of lime mortar (it's easiest to buy ready mixed and matured lime plaster that's been specially blended for use as backing coat plaster), 'tease' in the measured amount of animal hair (horse or cow usually), avoiding big clumps, (again, buy it from the same supplier and follow the instructions). Mix thoroughly again, adjusting the consistency until its smooth and flowing well. Not too wet and not too dry.

NOTE: although some conservation pros advocate the use of a proper 'mortar mill' for lime mortars, a conventional cement/concrete drum type mixer is perfectly good enough for smaller quantities. I prefer the electric versions because you can easily switch them on and off making it easy to test for consistency, add hair, and cleaning out afterwards etc. You can even use a mixing attachment on a powerful drill and a bucket for small amounts.

## FIRST COAT

- Before applying the new plaster to the laths, make sure they look damp but are not actually dripping.

- Push a first coat (called the 'pricking up coat' or sometimes 'scratch coat') of haired lime mortar up, onto the lath and through the gaps using a plastering trowel and a hawk.

- Ensure around half the mortar goes through the gaps in between the laths (thus forming a strong mechanical key), half will then go underneath the laths and half will go on the floor, (I know, I know; that doesn't add up, but I'm just telling you how it feels, you'll know what I mean once you get started!).

- For the best quality work place small dabs or strips of plaster at intervals, carefully measured and levelled beforehand. These act as 'screeds' to work from.

- Work on small areas radiating out from your first area. It's not critical to get this coat perfect, just aim for a consistent thickness straight from the trowel. Aim for 10mm (3/8") or so underneath the laths. Flatten the plaster out as you go but don't over work this coat as you might damage the sensitive 'green' keys you've pushed through the laths.

- Once this first coat has started to harden off (time varies on temperature and humidity, a few hours generally), gently scratch up the surface to provide a key for the next coat. You can use a special 'comb' type pronged scratcher, or make one from stiff wire or by nailing three short lengths of lath together after cutting one end of them to a sharp point. Spread the laths out like a small fan and gently create wavy lines in the surface of the mortar at 45 degrees both ways to the laths, creating a rough diamond shaped pattern. Not too deep and never through to the laths. Adjust the laths to ensure all three are creating the same depth scratches.

- Allow the scratch coat to dry out. This varies and can take up to four weeks, depending upon temperature and humidity. A week or two is normal. Don't worry about any light shrinkage or cracking and don't try to 'correct' them, there's no need and you'll likely damage those all-important, delicate keys on top.

- Slow is good when allowing the scratch coat to dry out. Keep humidity high and draughts out.

- It's ready when you can't dent the surface with your thumb. The surface should still be slightly damp and usually only needs a fine spray of water from your garden sprayer before applying the second coat. If too dry keep wetting it until the surface stays damp looking.

**SECOND COAT**

Once the first coat is quite firm but not bone dry, it's ready for the second or 'floating coat' (sometimes called the 'brown coat' or even 'straightening coat'). Damp down the first coat the day before and shortly before applying the second coat. Again, the plaster should be damp but not actually wet/dripping etc.

Knock up your lime mortar and trowel it on around on 6mm (1/4") or so on top of the first coat spreading and flattening it out as you apply it.

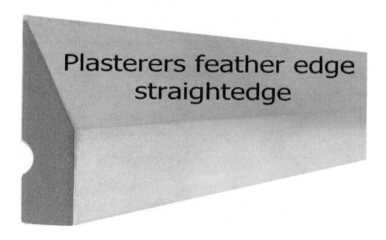

Plasterers feather edge straightedge

Once you have completed a small area, (say a square yard or metre) use a plasterer's aluminium feather edge board and run it over your newly plastered area both ways to 'rule it' flat. This smooths out the plaster, taking away the high spots and filling in the low spots.

- Top quality work requires small dabs or strips of plaster placed at intervals, carefully measured and levelled. These act as 'screeds' to work or 'rule' from with your straight edge, dragging or 'sawing' the excess plaster away in areas.

- Hair in this second coat appears to be down to choice, some do and some don't! Personally, I don't see the harm and add it, (but maybe in a little less quantity than in the first coat).

- Once this second coat has started to harden off (time varies on temperature and humidity, a few hours generally) this second coat needs to be thoroughly 'scoured' to further compact and flatten out the mortar. This is the process of working in a circular motion using a wooden float gently pressing and rubbing at the same time. This will work up a little softness in the surface, removing mortar from remaining high spots and rubbing it into the low spots. You may need to add little 'gobs' of mortar here and there as you notice little circles in the surface pointing out especially low spots. Splash a little water onto the surface if it's dry in places (but not too much).

- Usually the edges of the ceiling and areas near windows and doors will be ready slightly before the centre, but the wet stuff will let you know as the float drags and digs in the stuff that's too wet and skates over too dry areas.

- Once the scoured second coat has hardened off a little more (time varies on temperature and humidity, a fairly short time generally) gently scratch up the surface to provide a fine key for the final coat. Usually with a wooden float with 4 or 5 nails only just protruding from its base (called a 'devils float'). You don't want it as deep as the first time, just small shallow scores to give a little key for the final plaster.

## FINISH COATS

- Once the second coat is 'green' dry (varies again from a few days to a week or so) it's ready for the finish coat or 'setting coat'. This is applied in two (or sometimes three) very thin layers.

- Damp down and trowel on a thin coat (2mm or 1/16") of the fine finish plaster, (it's made from mixing lime putty with a blend very fine sand) followed shortly after (wet on wet) with a second similar coat, trowelling it out, flat and smooth as you go. You'll probably just have time for a cup of coffee in between the two coats...

- Once the finish coats have 'set up' after a short time (ranges from a few minutes to an hour or more) trowel up the surface using a little water where necessary to pull up a little 'fat' to move around, filling in imperfections.

- Alternatively, a rub a well rung out sponge over the surface of the surface until you get the texture you like. Some folks like the ceramic tillers grouting 'sponge on a float' type tool for this and they are effective, if not authentic!

- After a week or so, a coloured lime wash is usually applied as final decoration.

# REMOVING LATH AND PLASTER

*This ceiling is ready for the town dump, but hey, it's taken almost 300 years to get into this kind of condition...*

U h oh.....so you've made the difficult decision to take your ceiling down hmm? Don't feel bad, if your ceilings are economically beyond repair and you need to run new piping for radiators etc. or new wiring for downlights, new power points etc, it's an understandable decision. Luckily, it's not all bad news, taking down lath and plaster is a perfect DIY project, even for relative beginners. However, be prepared, it's quite hard work and very, very messy! But first, here's what you're going to need to get your ceiling on the floor...

## TOOLS AND EQUIPMENT

Fortunately, you don't need many, and you may already have most of them in your tool kit.

- PPE or personal protection equipment. Eye protection, dust mask, gloves and a disposable coverall (like the forensic guys wear...) with a hood is the way to go.

- A sturdy and safe working platform. Builder's trestles with scaffold planks are best, or at least a pair of sturdy stepladders (or two with a plank between them).

- Claw hammer or other light hammer.

- For stripping the mortar/plaster off and away from the lath you'll need a gauging or brick trowel (for removing very soft plaster) and/or a garden spade (for removing tougher stuff).

- Metal bar to lever with (crowbar, wrecking bar, pry bar etc.).

- Pick axe (optional but useful for getting the laths down) or a special 'rough neck' or 'pallet breaker' bar especially for removing things from joists.

- Clean up gear. Shovel, sweeping brush, dustpan, wheelbarrow etc and a powerful 'shop' vacuum cleaner (preferably not the 'other half's' best one!).

## OPTIONAL GEAR

- Dust protection such as polythene and dustsheets.

- Rubble sacks (or Gorilla style tubs/trugs).

- Electrical screwdrivers for removing old light fittings.

- Temporary lighting if required.

- Ventilation fans (optional but nice).

## LIGHTING

Unless you're the nocturnal type, or you're doing the job in bright daylight, you'll need to think about how you're going to see what you're doing. Don't forget that you'll have removed any lights in the ceiling beforehand and made safe any exposed wiring (put any bare wire ends into separate terminal blocks and cover with insulation tape (don't forget to isolate the supply first, duh!).

I adore the WAGO style wiring connector to make wiring safe. Remember these are connected inside, so never mix wire colours in these unless you like loud bangs and the thrill of risking your life...

## WAGO reusable electrical connectors.

Simply lift up the orange spring loaded lever, pop the 10mm bare ends of your wire into the hole and snap the lever down to connect.

**Simple, quick and safe.**

Once the room has been cleared and sheeted down (if applicable), install some temporary lighting. Floodlights seem to be a common choice for many, but they are terrible for 'blinding' you if you happen to glance directly at them, so if you have choice, fluorescent type lamps give you a better light without blinding (as well as being more robust against occasional knocks).

## VENTILATION

Bit obvious this one, but you are going to make a lot of dust and creating a way of getting it out of the room will make your working conditions much better. An open window as a minimum. If you have access to an old fan, you can prop it in the window, facing out and use it as a crude extract fan to get the air moving out of the room. Oh, and don't forget your dust mask, you'll still need one, even if you're using ventilation fans.

## THE MESS...

*Did I mention removing a lath and plaster can get a little bit messy..........?*

Before you start please consider... "THE MESS"

It gets messy?......Oh yeah. It gets really, really, really messy. Seriously, it makes so much dust that you should remove everything from the room and seal off the doors with masking tape before you start. Oh, and in case you were wondering, the above kitchen was coming out. You can also just make out the trestles which, when coupled with scaffold battens made a perfect working platform for removing this high ceiling.

All that mess comes partially from the accumulated dust that's on top of your old plasterwork and from within the plasterwork itself as it crumbles into powder on removal. The dust is very fine in particle size and it gets everywhere, really, I mean it, everywhere!

If you have built in stuff that you just can't remove, cover it down with thin polythene taped at the joints and edges. In addition, don't forget the door into the room. You can buy zippered polythene temporary doors to tape over the doorframe or simply tape two overlapping pieces of polythene over the doorway to 'climb' thorough.

Polythene is good because the dust is often fine enough to go through the average dustsheet. I personally discovered that little gem as a young apprentice; you don't want to know how...

## THINGS TO WATCH OUT FOR

### PIPES

Many pipes live in the unseen spaces in your home, including behind your ceiling, possibly. It's not terribly likely that pipes will be sitting on top of the laths; most often, you'll find them cut into the top of the joists or running through holes in the middle some-where. However, in really old houses pipes are always retro fitted of course, and not always in a logical place. Pipes don't often pose a problem because they're usually rigid enough to support their own weight, just be careful not to catch them with a saw (modern pipes are surprisingly thin walled) or pull them about lest you break a joint.

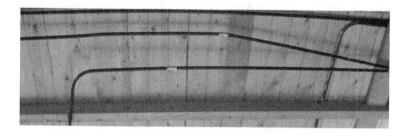

Make sure you know how to isolate the water supply though, just in case... seriously. I've seen a burst pipe or two in my time and the amount of water from even the tiniest hole will shock you with its intensity and volume...

Definitely not the time to wonder (a) What is a stopcock? (b) Where is the stopcock? and (c) Is it seized up from disuse? (Quite common on old, neglected stop cocks). Talking of stopcocks. Never leave a stopcock fully open. Always open it until it stops; then turn it back (closing it) half a turn (then it's much less likely to seize/stick over time).

## WIRES/CABLES

Wires or cables live alongside the pipes in the unseen spaces above your ceilings. Keep a look out for them as they drop out of the ceiling when you remove the laths. Tack nails to the side of the joists and cable tie the wires back up and out of harms way. Don't pull or otherwise stress them, lest they come out of their fittings. You'd think that electricians pay for cable by the millimetre judging by how tight some cable runs are! Obviously, be especially careful where you *know* there will be wires, e.g. around the ceiling light rose, switches or where there are electrical sockets etc.

## INSULATION

Mostly in the form of a thick 'woolly' blankets made from fibreglass or wool. It's often old, dirty and dusty stuff that you definitely don't want to get down your neck. Handle any insulation you find as if it's going to explode; i.e. slowly and at arm's length! If your ceilings are old enough to need replacing it's likely that the insulation is also past its best, so remove it, bag it up and fit new, thicker, more effective insulation in its stead. Be especially careful of loose or 'blown' insulation, which can literally pour through any holes you make in the ceiling, like water down a plughole. Always remove loose insulation from above if you're taking down the laths (if possible).

## NESTS

Mice nests are common above old ceilings or in joist spaces. Look for piles of shredded soft material, like newspapers, boxes, insulation, fabric or anything remotely chewable really.

Squirrel nests are rare, but we found one that must have started soon after the house's completion in 1722, (judging by its size); it was over 6 feet (1.8m) across! Generations of squirrels were getting into the loft space and building their version of the Taj Mahal.

You might find bee and wasp nests too, once I found a nest totally filling the space between a pair of floor joists where the bees had found holes in the cladding. It looked like a huge pile of stripy brown whipped cream!

## SKELETONS

No, not the 'in the closet' kind or the 'under-the-floorboards' kind, (although anything is possible.... Sorry, scaring you now!) However, skeletal remains of dead animals are not unusual. You might find the bones of mice or rats that have died from old age or after eating poison laid out by previous owners. On one project, we found a derelict loft complete with dozens of skeletal pigeons! In addition, a colleague of ours swears he found a mummified cat once in between some joists....

## RUBBLE TROUBLE

Rubble from earlier work is common. When tradesmen take up floorboards to install new pipes or wiring, they often make a mess (shocking huh!) and guess where this mess often ends up? Yup, swept through the holes in the floor where it sits on top of the ceiling below waiting for you to bash a hole through the ceiling, where upon it proceeds to pour all over you. Be especially careful if your home has had new roof tiles at some point. We found one loft space where the roofers had left many broken slates and lots of old mortar sitting on top of the bedroom ceilings after replacing the roof underlay and tiles.

## STORED ITEMS

There shouldn't be anything sitting on top of the ceiling itself (normally stuff is stored on top of the ceiling joists, on boards preferably) but sometimes people don't know (or care) and you'll see old, long forgotten or abandoned junk sitting on top of the ceiling itself. If possible, always check above the ceiling you're removing before you get started.

## INTERESTING AND CURIOUS STUFF

Old newspaper is always a delight to find. Often used to stuff in gaps or cracks etc. and covered over by folks renovating their home. Newspaper offers a little insight into the history of your home, such as dates of repairs, alterations or additions. The same goes for old cigarette packets and the like, left behind by tradesmen, often found under floors and above ceilings.

For some reason tradesmen also went through a phase of leaving adult magazines in hidden spaces...

Also, look out for notes left behind by bored or humorous tradesmen. We often find notes, comments, dates etc. written in the hidden spaces above ceilings etc. They vary from "the tradesman's name" up to "what the heck are you doing in here?" type comments, often signed and dated by the tradesman. I've even found a plumber's business card stapled to the side of a joist near a relatively new pipe run (which I thought was quite entrepreneurial!)

## HEALTH AND SAFETY (DON'T YOU DARE JUMP OVER THIS PART!)

I know, I know, you don't want to hear it; health and safety, yada, yada, yada. But listen up; there are a few things you must to do to get your ceiling down without needing to take time off work because you've hurt yourself, OK? And don't worry, it's only a short list...

- Clear the room. When you're working overhead, you can't see your feet (unless you're really freaky). Don't stumble around and fall over, clear the room of ALL non-essential stuff.

- Work from a sturdy base. The higher the ceiling the better the platform needs to be. A sturdy stepladder might be fine for an 8 foot (2.4m) ceiling but you're going to need a platform (see next) for anything 10 foot (3m) and over.

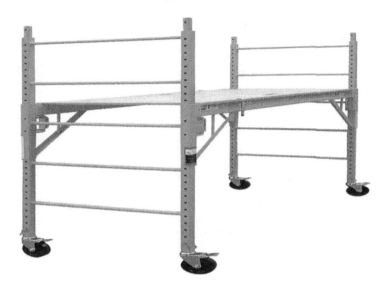

Protect your eyes with a set of safety glasses. Debris flies all over when taking down a ceiling. Lath in particular is springy stuff and when one 'lets go' it slingshots little bits of mortar and grit at high speed towards.... Yup, you. Goggles are best, but any kind of glasses are better than nothing.

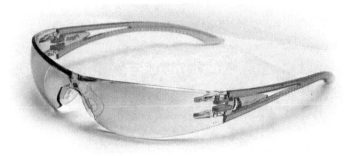

Protect your lungs; preferably with a proper respirator, (they are not terribly expensive). Get one with replaceable filters. Removing lath and plaster makes a LOT of fine dust that you really don't want inside you. Disposable masks should be a last resort, but they won't stop nearly enough, trust me.

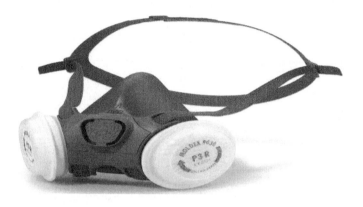

Protect your hands with gloves. Laths are brittle, sharp and splintery and old mortar will really dry out and roughen up your hands. If you don't want to snag your stockings (or anyone else's), wear gloves. Rubber 'criss-cross' gloves as a minimum, but well-fitting leather/hide gloves are best.

A protective coverall with a hood will keep the worst of the mess out. Sure, they can be a little warm to wear, but the alternative is everything you wear ending up covered in fine black dust, inside and out. The shower will run black like you've been down a coalmine if you don't wear one.

Right, enough preparation, gird your loins my dears, it's time to go in like a boss...

# REMOVING YOUR CEILING STEP BY STEP

Lath and plaster ceilings are best removed from underneath, in six distinct stages. I should note that it's possible to remove a ceiling from above if you have access (from the attic for the top floor and after removing the floorboards for lower floors). However, removing them from above is much more dangerous and creates a mess that's much harder to clear up, but I'll include a note about it a little later, (if you absolutely insist on doing it!).

OK, assuming you've read the first part of this chapter and just to refresh your memory...

- Clear everything out of the room.

- Cover down anything you want to protect and keep.

- Set up a safe working platform.

- Gather up all the tools you'll need.

- Remove any electrical fittings etc. that are in the way and set up some temporary lights.

- Open windows/ outside doors and/or set up a fan etc.

- Don your personal protection equipment (PPE).

Then you're ready for the first step, to remove all three coats of plaster.

### STEP ONE: REMOVE THE PLASTER

Start with the worst looking area (it's probably the weakest/ easiest), or wherever is convenient really! Work in front or to the side of yourself (whichever feels most comfortable or natural), use a claw hammer (or similar) to tap the plasterwork in a small circle until it breaks up and falls away. Keep going until you have exposed a small area of the underlying lath; let's say an area 300mm x 300mm (12" x 12"). Now you can see exactly how the ceiling is constructed, (which is interesting, yes?).

Next is to find which tool is going to work best to remove the rest of the plaster. On some ceilings (poorly constructed, or very old or badly damaged ones), you'll find the plaster doesn't need much encouragement to fall off. Let's face it, the reason you're removing it, is because it's in bad shape and don't forget gravity is on your side (which is why you're working in front or to one side of yourself...).

If the plaster falls away easily, try sliding a stout trowel between the lath and the plaster in as far as it will go and lever it downwards. If it's a bit tougher, try the same thing with a wrecking/crow bar, or even the claw part of your hammer. Sometimes you can remove huge areas of plaster in one go using a strong garden spade, which is my personal weapon of choice for easily removing plaster. A spade also has two secondary benefits, they are long enough to give good leverage and also to remove yourself from underneath the falling plaster. Smart.

Working out from your initial hole, strip off the plaster following the direction of the lath until you hit a wall. Then work sideways a little, reverse direction and work your way back across the ceiling. Rinse and repeat. If the plaster comes off really easily you can try working across the direction of the laths (sometimes their unevenness snags the tool making it harder work) If working in all directions works, then by all means radiate out from your first hole taking as much plaster off as you can reach with your chosen tool.

You'll be making a lot of noise and mess at this point, with the plaster raining down all around you kicking up lots of dust. I know, it's not a nice job, but it always has to get worse before it can get better. Just think of that beautiful new ceiling you're going to have in the end...

Once all the plaster is on the floor, get the heck out of there, go and grab some fresh air and a cup of coffee, you'll be ready for one, plus it'll give the dust time to settle.

## STEP TWO: CLEAR UP THE PLASTER

Back so soon? My my, you are keen! Right then, before taking down the laths it's **imperative** to clear away the fallen plaster at the end of step one, because if you don't, you'll end up with huge pile of lath reinforced plaster that's very, very difficult to clear up. You'll also find it difficult (and dangerous) to move your stepladder or working platform around the room with plaster all over the floor. You don't need to sweep up necessarily, just aim to get all the big stuff picked up and cleared away using a shovel. I'm amazed how many folks try to pull the whole ceiling down on one go, stumbling all over the place on a big pile of mixed up debris. In addition, today many recycling places require you to sort out your waste before dumping it anyway. Wooden laths need to go into a burn or compost container and the plaster into a 'hardcore' or bulk landfill container for example.

NOTE: When clearing up, *please take your time*, if you work slowly and carefully you will cause less dust to 'go airborne'. Slide the shovel slowly under the rubble, lift it gently, being careful not to spill stuff off the side of the shovel and gently put it into the bucket/sack slowly sliding the rubble off. Whereas, if you rush about slinging the stuff all over the place, the room will quickly fill up with dust again. If you're lucky enough to be working on a 'yet to be finished' floor you can use a garden sprayer to damp down the plaster on the floor before picking it up (damp dust is too heavy to go airborne). If you have a companion, get them to spray a very fine mist in the air on and just above where you are shovelling up the plaster, which further minimises the dust.

**STEP THREE: REMOVE THE LATHS**

Now you have a clear floor, the next step is to remove the laths. You'll probably manage just fine removing them with your claw hammer or possibly a wrecking or crow bar. Simply lever them off and don't worry about the nails at this stage, they rarely come out. If you have a 'pick axe' (of all things!) slide the blade through a few laths and then place the head of the pickaxe onto the bottom of a joist and lever down large sections of laths. In the UK, laths are thin, brittle, riven or split hardwood, which usually causes them to break into smallish sections, leaving the nails behind in the joist. Some countries use a sawn lath, which are a little stronger and may come off in longer lengths.

Pull all the laths down with whatever tool you have to hand that works best for you.

I know I mentioned the dreaded H & S issues earlier, but this is the part where you're most likely to hurt yourself. Laths are very strong and springy and there'll be lots of debris clinging to them. When you try to lever them away, they nearly always snap and fling bits all over the place; eye protection is essential, even if you're a tough guy.

NOTE: Some folks say it's easier to take out the nails at the same time as taking down the laths and if you want to, that's fine. I do it separately because I like to use a pickaxe to take down the laths and I don't want to be swapping tools every few seconds. Moreover, I like to focus solely on removing nails and checking the condition of each joist methodically, there's less risk of me missing a nail or other problem that way.

## STEP FOUR: CLEAR UP THE LATHS AND PLASTER KEYS

Once all the laths are on the floor, you'll notice that there's a load of bits of plaster too. Where the heck did they come from, I thought we'd cleared up all the plaster? Ah, no. Remember earlier where we talked about those mortar keys, nibs or snots that squeezed through the gaps in the laths during the plastering to hold it all up? Yup those, well they were sitting on top of the laths, usually under a few decades, or even centuries of dust. And now, here they are again, all over the floor.

Starting with the laths, gather them all up into buckets, bags or a wheelbarrow ready for disposal. You'll find that laths are brilliantly, spectacularly splintery, just right for sticking into soft (and even battle-scarred hands). Gloves are mandatory, and yes, even 'real men' wear gloves when clearing up laths...

One good method is to throw the laths into a tall 25L bucket, because that seems to stack them into an automatic bundle. Then lay a length of thin rope on the ground and carefully slide the laths halfway out of the bucket over it and tie it all up in a neat bundle ready for disposal etc.

If you have a wood burner though, or just like building fires outdoors to toast your marshmallows on, then by all means snap the laths into 300mm (foot) long pieces, because for sure they make the best kindling there is...

That just leaves the plaster, again. As you did in step two, roughly clear away it away. Don't forget, you don't need to sweep up, just aim to scrape/ pick up the big pieces of plaster using your shovel.

**STEP FIVE: REMOVE THE OLD NAILS**

Right, working from your nice clear floor it's time to remove all those corroded nails and check the condition of the joists. For some reason folks often dread this step because there are usually hundreds, if not thousands of nails left behind in the joists. But hey, even if it's a little boring, it's an easy step to do (take your breaks where you find 'em!). The reason it's tedious and time consuming is because the nails are probably corroded. The nails corrode because there's moisture in the joists/ plasterwork, plus there are natural acids present in wood, which slowly attack unprotected metal. There were no rustproof nails back in those days remember. This corrosion causes the nail to expand a little (or a lot!) which really holds them in place.

There are ~~three~~ four options with old lath nails...

- Occasionally you'll be able to pull them out with your claw hammer or pry bar.

- Sometimes they snap off with a sideways blow from your claw hammer.

- At times, it's easier just to hammer them all the way in.

●》— And now and then, you'll use a mixture of all three on one nail!

You'll work out what's best for your nails quickly enough through trial and error once you get started.

NOTE: Get into the habit of dragging the side of your hammerhead along the joist every few nails, (to make sure you don't miss any). Oh, and you *really* don't want to miss any, not even one. Believe me; you will curse when you're holding up a drywall board and there's a nail sticking out of a joist, preventing the board from going up properly. It's difficult enough manoeuvring a heavy drywall board over your head once, let alone twice!

I like to examine the joists whilst I am removing the nails. Soft areas of rot will sound dull when tapped with a hammer, whereas good timber gives a pleasing 'thunk'. Poking with an old screwdriver is a good idea if you're not sure and don't worry, you'll not hurt the joist...

Also, whilst your there, look for any white, salty stains that might indicate water leaks. Lastly, look for insect damage (think woodworm); investigate any small holes or tracks. I'll probably mention this again in the chapter 'Installing Drywall', because it'd be a shame to miss a problem at this late stage.

### STEP SIX: FINAL CLEARING UP

Guess what, there's debris on the floor again. In this debris, you'll find the nails you just pulled/ knocked out and probably lots of dust left over from the rough clearing up you did earlier. You can probably use a sweeping brush this time and the fine water spray from the garden sprayer if you found it worked for you (not too much water at this stage though or it'll turn into mud!). Again, as with the shovel work/ sweep slowly to minimise dust being flicked up into the air.

You'll probably want to finish off with an old vacuum cleaner to clean up the last of the dust. Don't use your best vacuum cleaner though, because this dust is very fine (compared to everyday dust). If you *must* use your best cleaner, bang out the air filter/screen very regularly (every 5 minutes) and empty it the second it starts straining the motor to prevent it overheating.

By design, domestic vacuums just can't handle construction dust and you'll easily kill yours if you don't follow this advice. BTW, many vacuums have a overheat cut-out function so if your vacuum suddenly stops, unplug it and leave it to cool down for a while. Clean the filter, empty/change the bag and try again (you might be lucky).

*Dusty? Little bit. Probably time to grab another cup of coffee.*

## REMOVING A CEILING FROM ABOVE

I promised I'd briefly mention this as it's a popular method if you have easy access to the ceiling from above (either from inside the attic space or if the floorboards have been taken up). Just remember it's dangerous, especially for anyone not used to scampering about on joists. If you've ever put your foot through a bedroom ceiling whilst in the attic, this is probably not the method for you!

Working from above simply push the whole lath and plaster ceiling down into the room below, using a heavy spade/ shovel or a sledgehammer held vertically as a crude 'battering ram' or even your boots (make sure you hold onto something or someone though). Simply hit the back of the laths close to and either side of the joists with your preferred tool (a long handled 3.5kg or7lb sledgehammer works well). Keep a firm hold on the tool though, dropping these hammers a few feet can do a lot of damage to the floor.

Although I can see the merit of working from above, it's easier work and less mess lands on you (and I have been involved during this numerous times). It's just so inherently dangerous I can't recommend it, because it's all too easy to fall through the joists when you're concentrating on knocking down the ceiling. Jumping around safely on 'open joists' requires years of practice. I once saw a labourer slip and fall either side of a pair of joists that still had old-fashioned cut floorboard nails sticking up out of them.... A pair of these nails cruelly ripped the inside of his upper leg to ribbons. Did he scream? Not half.

I also find the resulting heap of debris *very* difficult to clear away, because the lath and plaster become so impossibly tangled and mixed up that separating them is very time consuming. Arguably losing much of the time saved by kicking the ceilings down quickly from above.

## LEVELLING UP CEILINGS

Before replacing your ceiling, you'll need to decide whether you are happy for the new ceiling to simply follow the original timber work, come what may, OR whether you want to make the new ceiling completely flat and/or level. It depends on the look you are aiming for (traditional higgledy-piggledy cottage, or minimalistic modern chic etc).

For the cottage look just go right ahead and skip this chapter! But some folks like their new ceilings perfectly flat and level. The most popular ways to flatten a ceiling are...

### SISTER THE EXISTING JOISTS

Sistering (made up word!) means adding new, straight and level timbers onto the side of and slightly below the bottom of the original joists, thus levelling up any unevenness etc.

- Gluing and screwing new timber onto the existing joists helps to reinforce them.

- Minimum thickness of 25mm (1") if you are a good shot with drywall screws. More common is to use 38mm (1 ½") or even 50mm (2") wide timber.

🔩— The depth of the new timber depends on your joists. It doesn't need to be full height and as little as 100mm (4") is common if it's just to level up the ceiling. However, if you're trying to reinforce poor joists, try to get as close to full height as possible.

Existing, bowed ceiling joists

New 'sistered' timber screwed alongside

## ADD PACKED CROSS BATTENS.

Cross battens are small timbers fastened underneath the ceiling, either at 90 degrees to the joists or directly underneath them.

🔩— Batten size depends on your available head height, 50mm x 50mm (2" x 2") is common, but down to 25mm x 50mm (1" x 2") is also OK.

🔩— Starting from the lowest corner first. Place the first batten on the ceiling and drive in the first screw all the way up tight (because it's the lowest point).

- Work along this batten using your spirit level, inserting thin 'shims' or packers above the batten before tightening up each screw. You now have a level and straight batten.

- Very carefully, transfer the bottom edge of each end of the above batten across to the opposite side of the room. This tells you where this batten needs to go in order for the ceiling to be level. God bless laser levels huh? What, you don't have a laser level? Quick, before the store closes, go and buy one. A cheapo one will do, you'll never regret it for a second and you'll wonder how you managed without one... (measure up from the laser line to the ends of your first batten and then repeat at the other end of the room, marking the top of your tape).

- Fasten the second batten up to the joists with the appropriate shims to ensure a level batten perfectly in line with your new pencil marks.

- Now, here's the clever bit to help you fix all the intermediate battens. Fasten a very tight string line up (or just use a straight edge) between your newly fastened battens over where you want the other battens to go. At each fastening point measure the gap between the string (or straight edge) and the ceiling.

- Take away the thickness of your batten and that's the size 'shim' you need. For example, say it measures 38mm (1½") from string to ceiling and you're using 25mm (1") battens then 38-25=13, therefore you need a 13mm (1/2") shim. Pin each shim to the ceiling along the lines where you're eventually going to screw up the battens.

- This avoids the risk of mistakes caused by battens touching the string line and pushing it down, making subsequent battens incorrect.

- Either make your own shims using a table saw to rip down some scrap timber or buy plastic ones (1mm, 2mm, 5mm and 10mm are useful sizes to have), use small squares of plastic DPC (damp-proof-course) for micro shims, less than 1mm, if you're really particular... (like me!)

- Once all the shims are pinned to the ceiling, remove the string lines and simply screw up all the remaining battens, through the pinned shims, secure in the knowledge that they are perfectly in line and level with the first two battens.

NOTE: Don't forget to allow for the shim thickness when calculating your screw lengths (batten depth+ shim+ 38mm (1 ½")) joist penetration; rounded up to the next available screw size), for example, a 25mm/ 1" (batten) + 10mm/ 3/8" (shim) + 38mm (1 ½") (joist) = 73mm (2 7/8") so a 75mm (3") minimum screw size.

NOTE: You can of course do all the above using your new laser level, but the maths is a little more complicated as you have the height from the laser to the underside of the lath to minus as well as the batten thickness.

- Use the 'new space' to run cables and/or pipes etc.

- Insulate the new space if required.

## REPLACE WARPED JOISTS.

Occasionally a ceiling looks bad because one or two joists have rotted, dried twisted or sagged out of shape, pushing the ceiling down. It's not too difficult to cut out and replace individual joists in their entirety...

- Make sure there are no loads on the floorboards above if applicable (i.e. move beds, drawers, wardrobes etc.).

- Remove and replace one joist at a time for safeties sake, unless additional supports are used.

- Remove any strutting or solid blocking between the joists (cut through them and twist them out).

- Remove the joist by cutting it out in sections and twisting it out or using pairs of wrecking bars.

- Push up or cut off any nails protruding through the floorboards above.

- Enlarge the hole in the wall at one end to easily facilitate the installation of the new joist.

- Pencil mark the new joist at 100mm (4") in from each end to ensure you have adequate bearing in the wall.

- Slide the joist into the larger hole, lift up into place and then slide back into the hole at the other end.

- Mortar and/or brick up the spaces around the new joist ends. Take the time to ensure gaps are full.

- Re-fasten the floorboards above (if applicable).

- Replace any strutting (herringbone or solid) or consider installing some if it's missing.

# Different types of strutting to stabilise floor joists

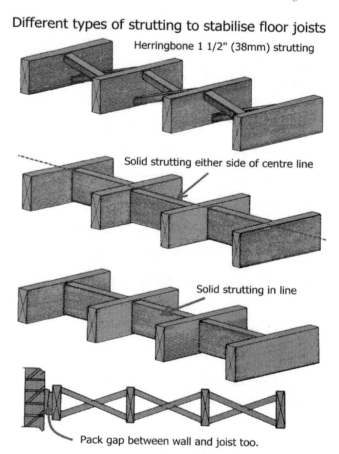

Herringbone 1 1/2" (38mm) strutting

Solid strutting either side of centre line

Solid strutting in line

Pack gap between wall and joist too.

# INSTALLING DRYWALL

*This ceiling is ready for boarding.... once the dust has settled!*

I nstead of repeating this several times throughout this book, I'll explain how to install drywall here. These principles are broadly similar whether you are over-boarding a ceiling, boarding onto battens or going straight onto the newly exposed joists.

## BEFORE YOU START

If you didn't do the following list at the removing the old nails stage, take a few moments to run through it now. Because it'd be a shame to find a problem after you've started the actual drywall installation...

- Whilst you have good access to everything, take a powerful light source and check everywhere for signs of damage...

- Look for soft areas of rot, tapping with a hammer or poking with an old screwdriver, you'll hear/ feel it (because it'll sound different to the good areas) .

- Look for white stains which might indicate water leaks (salty deposits form when moisture evaporates).

- If you haven't already, look for insect damage (think wood-worm), investigate any small holes or tracks.

- If your ceiling joists have any 'trimmed' areas (around a chimney or staircase for example); take photographs of the joist layout, because anything not logical or obvious has a nasty habit of 'disappearing' from your mind once you have lifted the drywall up into place and covered it up. Record any new pipe or cable runs too for future maintenance or alterations.

Lastly but most importantly...

- Remember to put vertical pencil marks on the wall to indicate where the centre of each joist is. This makes finding your joists so much easier when you are boarding. Make sure you mark the wall below the thickness of the drywall or you'll not see them once the board is in place!

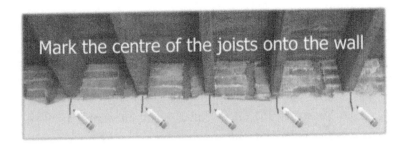

## CHOOSING DRYWALL VARIETIES.

Call into your local supplier for a brochure and to see what they keep in stock. If they need to order it in, the chances are it's not a popular choice in your area. The stuff that's in stock is what the majority of folks are using.

Arguably the 2.4m x 1.2m x 12.5mm (8' x 4' x ½") sheet is the most commonly used, but drywall is available in lots of different sizes and thicknesses. From super thin 6mm boards for renovation up to 15mm boards for ceilings with large joist spacing's etc. There are also boards made for lots of different situations such as...

- Sound blocking boards which are especially dense.

- Heat resistant boards for cladding fire sensitive parts of a structure (think steel beams etc.).

- Moisture resistant boards for wet areas.

- Insulated boards for minimising heat loss.

- Foil backed board to resist moisture penetration (good for kitchens and bathrooms) as it incorporates a vapor barrier.

- Impact resistant boards for high traffic areas (v. hard surface).

- Bendable boards for curved work.

- X-ray proof boards lined with lead, (no really!) for shielding medical machinery. Remember when your dentist disappears behind the wall?

## THERE ARE TWO TYPES OF DRYWALL...

I know I just said there were many different types of drywall available, but 90% of the time when you call into your local friendly builders' merchant, there's usually only two different types actually (different sizes apart)...

- Squared edge boards

- Tapered edge boards.

Which you choose depends on how you want to finish off your drywall, i.e. just the joints or the whole surface?

### TAPERED EDGE (FINISH JUST THE JOINTS AND SCREW HOLES)

Tapered edge boards are slightly thinner along the two long edges to allow you to stick tape (or glassfibre mesh) over the joints and fill them up with joint compound. In addition, you'll need to fill the screw holes and then you're good to go. These are common in the USA.

### SQUARE EDGED BOARDS (PLASTER THE WHOLE SURFACE)

Alternatively, there are regular square edged boards. To finish these, stick glassfibre joint tape over all the joints and then plaster or skim the whole surface with good or so with 3 or 4mm (1/8") of a special two-coat finish plaster. This is one of the most common boards in the UK.

## SETTING OUT DRYWALL

Because small pieces of drywall break easily during installation, you need to set out properly to avoid them where possible. Usually the long side of the drywall board goes across the joists. Think about the length and width of the room in relation to the size of the drywall boards you have and follow these tips...

- Measure across the room (along the joists) and divide this figure by the short side length of your boards. Aim to avoid a small cut on the other side of the room (say under 200mm or 8"). If you are going to end up with a small cut, reduce the width of the first board to give you a bigger cut the other side.

- Start the drywall along the longest, straight side of the room (usually).

- Start the first board either tight up or just a tiny distance away from said straight wall (my preference is to butt them up tight though).

- Carefully examine the end joint (short side) very carefully as you offer up subsequent boards; it must be either tight up or exactly parallel. If it's not, then the long edges of the boards are not in line/straight and this will cause tremendous problems as you add more boards.

- Again (it's important!), check that the first run of drywall boards is very, very straight, as it determines how the rest of the boards go up across the room. Mistakes here get worse as you work across the room, leading to uneven gaps between the boards (not a disaster but still, it doesn't help either...).

- Compete the first run next to the wall. On older houses with unusual joist spacing, you might find you need to cut every board to ensure the end joints centre over a joist. In this situation, I've seen folks slide lengths of 25 x 100mm (1" x 4") timber over the top of the joint to create 'flying joint's, but it's probably better to cut the boards over the middle of a joist.

- Cut the last board to fit up to the wall and see if the offcut is suitable to start the next run. Try to stagger the boards by two joists for best results.

- Start the next run of boards in a roughly 'half bond' pattern (like a brick wall). Butt the boards up tight if possible, although small gaps are not usually a problem and sometimes unavoidable on bumpy ceilings. Some folks insist that leaving the width of a matchstick gap all around boards makes for stronger joints once filled... We can argue about that one all day long!

- The third run of boards should mirror the first and the fourth mirrors the second, and so on across the room until you reach the other wall. Measure and cut to fit the last board to fill the gap up to the wall.

## CURVED OR WAVY WALLS

- To start on old wavy walls, measure out just less than a board's width and use a chalk line to mark a straight line on the joists underside to work to (adjust this to ensure a good size cut at the opposite side of the room). Ensure the distance from the line to the wall is less than the size of your drywalls short side at all points along the wall.

- Measure from the line to the wall every 300mm (foot) or so and scribe these measurements onto the drywall (remember your orientation! Sometimes it's easier to visualise by marking onto the back of the board). Join the dots using a short straight edge and pencil. Cut the outer edge of the drywall to the curve you just marked using an old wood saw or drywall saw.

NOTE: Work to your chalk line. Again, check that the edge facing the rest of the room is very straight as it determines how the rest of the boards go up across the room.

## FASTENING DRYWALL

- The most important tip when screwing drywall boards to timber is;... learning when to stop!

- Aim for less than around 200mm (8") between screws.

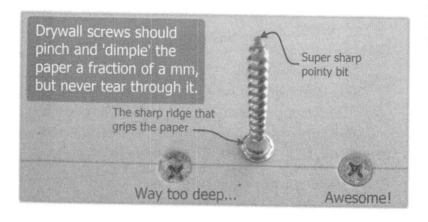

Drywall screws should pinch and 'dimple' the paper a fraction of a mm, but never tear through it.

Super sharp pointy bit

The sharp ridge that grips the paper

Way too deep...

Awesome!

NOTE: On a standard 1200mm (4') wide board. I'll put a screw at each side and one in the middle (which is usually marked with a faint line or line of text etc). Then it's easy to 'fill in' the gaps either side of the centre screw, dividing each space into three giving a spacing of around 200mm (8"). For some reason it's easier for the eye to equally divide up space between two objects than it is to measure a set length. Here, let's see if a picture explains it a little better...

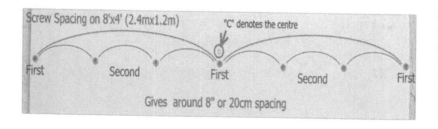

Screw Spacing on 8'x4' (2.4mx1.2m)

"C" denotes the centre

First    Second    First    Second    First

Gives around 8" or 20cm spacing

*A complicated way of explaining something simple!*

- On a paper bound edge, go no closer than 10mm (3/8") to the edge with screws.

- On a cut edge, go no closer than 13mm (1/2") to the edge with screws.

The easiest way to 'hang' drywall is to hire a mobile drywall jack or lift from your local tool hire store....

Just pop the drywall board onto the lift, tip it horizontal and wind it up to the ceiling.

Much easier than using your head and hands!

Contact your local tool hire store for details.

Using a lifting machine also avoids having to use tiny 900mm x 1200mm (3' x 4') boards if you're working alone. Remember that

Less joints makes for a better ceiling because there are less places for it to crack in the future.

- In a pinch you can make a pair of 'dead men' out of scrap timber to help hold the boards in place ready for fixing.

*Simple but effective, a 'dead man' offers a 'third hand'. Make them from scrap timber; measure a tiny bit more than from floor to joist height.*

## FINISHING DRYWALL

Because there are two main types of drywall there are two different ways of finishing them off, one finishes just the joints and screw holes and the other coats the entire surface of the boards with a thin 'veneer' of hard plaster. The choice is up to you and for every five people you find that swear by tapered edged boards, you'll find another five who insist that finish plaster is the best way. I'm from the UK where true drywall is not so common, so of course I lean towards the harder, superior finish that you'll get using a finish plaster, (but I'm not bias..... I do use tapered edge boards here in Norway!).

## TAPERED EDGE BOARDS

Cover the joints with a paper tape set in joint compound (traditional) or a self-adhesive glassfibre mesh strip (easier) before filling them up with several layers of joint compound over successive days. Fill the joints in three sessions usually, (maybe only two layers for screw holes).

When it comes to joint compound, there are many different sorts, but in the majority of cases for a DIY job, the standard all-purpose stuff is fine. Avoid anything that sets quickly (unless you know what you're doing) and make sure it's an 'easy to sand' version. Mix it up in the tub till it's smooth before using it on the first coat, but if you like, you can thin it a little for the subsequent coats to make it run little easier. Simply add a little water and mix it up using a 'potato' type masher or a paddle on a powerful electric drill, or at worst, a clean stick. You want a nice smooth and creamy consistency, but not too runny or soupy. Some folks describe it as somewhere between peanut butter and toothpaste if that helps! Proper drywall tools make the job easier and are worth the investment, as they'll save you hours of work and give you a superior finish.

- First coat, stick mesh over all the joints and run a strip of joint compound over the top or alternatively, set drywall tape into a thin layer of joint compound. Either way, smooth out and flatten the compound over the joint reinforcement using a wide bladed joint compound 'knife'.

- Fill all the screw holes. Dab and scrape!

- Second coat. The next day, fill the joint up to the top between the 'shoulders' of the tapered edge of the board with joint compound. Smooth out using a wide bladed joint compound 'knife'.

- Fill all the screw holes for the second time (they always shrink back a little).

- Third coat. The next day again, run a very thin coat to fill up any shrinkage in the joint and further feather the joint onto the boards either side. Smooth out the joint with the widest joint compound 'knife' you have.

- Some folks lightly brush the very edges of the compound with a damp sponge to remove any lines, ridges etc., although any small imperfections are easy to sand out afterwards.

- Once the final coat is fully dry (24hrs at least, longer in low temps.), sand the filled areas flat with 120-grit paper on a flat block or a sanding pad on a pole.

- Further light sanding with a 150-180 grit sandpaper is best for those wanting really top-quality results.

- The more care you took putting the compound on, the less sanding you'll need to do. Stick to the big brand jointing compounds, because some of the cheap ones are horrible to use and create more airborne dust.

## SHORT EDGES

The above applies to the long-tapered edges but what about the short sides that are not tapered for the compound? Well, it's basically the same as above, except the compound ends up slightly proud of the boards surface instead of inside the tapered recess. I'll not lie to you, this is tricky as you don't have the tapered edges to guide you, (I think boards should be tapered all round...).

In brief here is the or 'standard' or 'hard' way...

- Trim back the paper alongside the joint making sure it's perfect, most go for 'V' shape here. This is because the paper edge doesn't wrap around the edge and loose edges can be visible in the finished joint.

- Stick your joint mesh over the joint as normal (or bed your joint tape).

- Make even runs of compound either side of the mesh/tape, making sure the joint is full.

- Once the first coat is set, run a second slightly wider layer of compound over each side ensuring the mesh/tape over the joint is covered.

NOTE: Personally though, I create a slight depression on the short ends of drywall by using flying joints and shaped backing boards. I make my own backing boards out of OSB board cut on a table saw to create a 1.6mm (1/16") deep shallow V. There are various commercial solutions, just google "drywall butt backer" or "drywall butt board" to see pics of the principle.

NOTE: Tapered edge boards have large areas of the original paper visible, so it's important to use a special drywall sealer over the surface before decorating or the drywall will act like blotting paper, soaking up all your paint.

## SQUARE EDGE BOARDS

Square edged boards are completely flat so the entire surface of the boards needs covering in a finish or veneer plaster. The plaster is applied in two thin coats giving a thickness just around 3mm or 4mm (1/8" or so). It's a 'wet' process and is messy, depending on the tradesmen. Some are much messier than others let's say. Scaffolding or stilts are usually required to plaster a ceiling, as the wet plaster needs working over several times during and after application.

- Stick self-adhesive glassfibre tape over all joints.

- Thoroughly mix the powdered finish plaster until it's a very, very smooth, creamy consistency.

- Even a single lump in finish plaster is a nuisance. Site hygiene is important with finish plasters. Lumps in the mix will get large gobs of wet plaster thrown at you on site, along with some rather colourful vocabulary about your competence and parentage...

- Starting furthest away from any draughts (because open windows, doors etc. quickly dry out the plaster), apply the plaster to the boards in long even strokes using a plasterers hawk and a plastering trowel. The key is to apply it quite evenly, smoothing it out a little as you go, which is easier than it sounds because it's quite a thin coat.

- Wait a few minutes for the plaster to firm up a little (after a cup of coffee say). Then the second coat is applied 'wet on wet'. Professionals might 1st coat several walls before returning to 2nd coat the first one (but you'll need to be really fast and confident in your ability before copying this).

- Apply the second coat in the same manner as the first coat, although some plasterers choose to put this one on at 90 degrees to the first one.

- Once you have finished this second coat, it's a good idea for beginners to go back to the start and quickly run your trowel over it again to 'lay it in'. Watch the ceiling and see how the trowel is taking plaster from the high spots and depositing it in the low spots. Experiment with doing this at 90 degrees to the direction you applied it. This will hopefully make trowelling up a little easier before the plaster starts to set up, giving you a flatter ceiling.

- Next up lies the secret. Wait. You need to wait now until the plaster has firmed up just enough so that working it over with a trowel doesn't leave deep lines from the trowel edges.

- Start working on the plaster too soon and the plaster will stay soggy and you'll not manage to get the plaster flat without lots of lines.

- Leave it too long and you'll find it difficult because the plaster has set too hard to move/work.

- As you work the surface, the trowel should just pickup plaster from the high spots and deposit it into the low spots leaving the merest trace of trowel lines.

- With the plaster now flat, wait again for a few minutes. Once it's hardened off a little more, go over the plaster again with a wet trowel (have a big wet brush in your other hand). Wipe the trowel each time and even flick a little water onto the plaster on especially dry areas. The trowel shouldn't be picking up plaster at this point (well, not more than an occasional trace). The finish should be smooth and flat but not super glossy. So called 'polishing' is just not necessary (despite what the plasterers say).

No sanding is required on finish plaster, if it's done properly, in fact sanding will scratch the smooth surface the trowel made.

New plaster is very absorbent though, so it's a good idea to use a sealer on the plaster before hanging wallpaper. If painting, use water-based paint and either use a primer, or just thin down the first coat of paint a little (10% or so) to allow it to easily soak into the dry plaster.

# FAQ

*Here's just a selection of questions I've answered from my website over at handycrowd.com over the years...*

### IS MY CEILING GOING TO FALL DOWN AROUND MY EARS?

In my experience, ceilings are only rarely in danger of actually falling down. Even the bad ones only lose a few small bits of plaster from time to time. The ones to watch would be ceilings where there are additional factors in play, such as water leaks or structural problems etc. Nails rarely fail, even when corroded. This means the laths usually hold up just fine.

### HOW DO I FINISH OFF THE JUNCTION BETWEEN THE WALL AND THE CEILING?

Many period houses have a cornice, which hides these troublesome corners perfectly, but if your house doesn't have cornice, then using a good quality, flexible decorator's caulk will help. Avoid at all costs cheap caulk, it just isn't flexible enough and will shrink back and crack.

### WILL THIS WORK ON LATH AND PLASTER WALLS TOO?

Yes, what goes for ceilings pretty much goes for walls too. Although this guide is aimed at folks wanting to work on lath and plaster ceilings, exactly the same principles and methods are used to repair or remove it from walls too.

### DO I NEED TO SEAL THE OLD PLASTER BEFORE WALLPAPERING AND DECORATING?

You need a "primer sealer" to stabilise all that old dust. BUT, be careful if the 'dust' is white and salty as this could mean there is damp evaporating from the surface. Invest in a good brand of primer sealer and then use your regular wallpaper paste. Once sealed the wall will not 'suck out' the moisture in the paste too quickly, giving you time to work with the wallpaper.

## CAN I REMOVE THE CEILING BUT LEAVE THE CORNICE OR COVING IN PLACE?

The answer is: yes, you can remove the ceiling and leave the cornice or coving in place with a little bit of skill and a good dollop of luck. You'll just need to be especially careful on the two sides where the laths are at 90 degrees to the cornice, because the laths disappear underneath the cornice itself.

Where the laths run parallel to the cornice, the lath and plaster comes away much easier with a lot less risk to the cornice because you don't need to disturb the laths actually underneath the cornice.

The best way to cut through the plaster/laths is to use a Fein multi tool (Bosch make a cheaper version called the Multitool) which are useful for all sorts of other DIY things too! These tools have a really fine cut and don't disturb the cornice at all, if you work slowly and carefully. The main challenge being the high working height over your head.

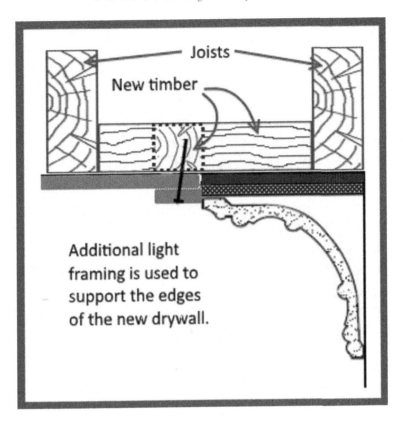

Joists

New timber

Additional light framing is used to support the edges of the new drywall.

Start by taking down the lath and plaster, going very carefully up to the cornice. Once close to the cornice, score the plaster at the front edge of the cornice a few times with a sturdy craft knife. Often the plaster breaks off cleanly and mostly flush with the cornice. If the plaster is tough though, don't force it; instead, use an abrasive blade in your 'multi' cutting tool to cut through just the plaster, stop when you hit the laths. Once the plaster is out of the way, swap the blade for a wood cutting one, which will last much longer if they only have laths to cut through. Cut the laths off as close to the cornice as you can get.

Depending on your ceiling joist configuration (and the size of the cornice), you will then have two extra hurdles to overcome...

First, where the cornice is parallel to the joists it's likely that there will be areas where there is nothing to screw the drywall boards to, because the first joist is behind the cornice.

Usually you can add a little light framing and 'nogging' out between the first and second joists and then in between the new noggings to give you something to fasten to (see pic above). I tend to use glue and thin gauge screws to fix the light framing in place as it's gentle, whereas wielding a hammer and nails will likely disturb the cornice.

Various packing pieces are likely in between the new framing and the existing laths over the cornice as it is often a little uneven in nature (fill thin gaps using a tube adhesive). After filling in any gaps, try to get some fasteners through the front edge of the cornice into the new timberwork to help replace the lost support from the laths. Very carefully drill and countersink holes though the cornice and use drywall screws into the timbers. NB! You need to have a real gentle touch for this, you're aiming to just hold the cornice in place, not pull it up tight (or at all actually) because that will break something and make matters worse. Once filled and sanded, you'll never know....

Second, the new drywall boards are likely to be thinner than the old lath and plaster work which can show up unsightly lath/plaster at the cornice edge. There are various ways to overcome this difference,

- Use 15mm (5/8th) drywall boards (after a plaster skimming coat and a little decorator's caulk you'll cover the edge on an average ceiling).

- Pack down the joists with thin timber pieces or even strips of 10mm (3/8th) drywall if it's an appropriate thickness when combined with the boards.

- Patch up above and behind the edge of the cornice and up to the new drywall boards with filler and caulk it (this depends on how clean the edges are and how thick the ceiling was).

One of my plasterer's (a great one!) sometimes adds a 75mm (3") strip of 10mm (3/8") drywall board around the edge of the ceiling boards (paper edge facing out) because the edge of the cornice was too thick. This had the effect (after painting) to make the cornice look much wider as the extra 75mm (3") of drywall looked like a part of the cornice instead of the ceiling. It does depend on the style of the cornice for this tip though. Still, it's very clever and looks like this...

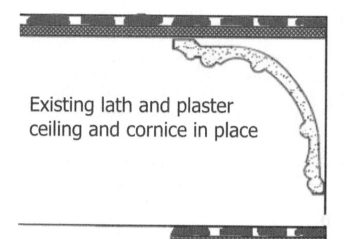

Existing lath and plaster
ceiling and cornice in place

Lath and plaster removed
up to cornice edge.

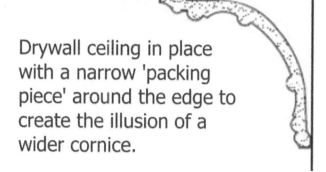

Drywall ceiling in place
with a narrow 'packing
piece' around the edge to
create the illusion of a
wider cornice.

Another alternative is to install the drywall on top (well technically it is underneath the lath; oh you know what I mean!) of the existing lath. This obviously retains the lath underneath the cornice (which is okay), but this solution really depends on how good/flat the existing laths are. One advantage of leaving the existing lath in place is that you can use board adhesive to strengthen up the edges of the drywall in front of the cornice, as it will squeeze through the lath just like the original plaster and hold it firmly in place.

# END NOTE

## ARE YOU READY FOR YOUR CEILINGS?

I hope I've managed to give you a good understanding of what's involved in repairing and/or taking down and replacing a lath and plaster ceiling. But most of all, I hope you're now fully inspired and motivated to have a go at repairing or replacing them yourself.

And REMEMBER... Don't panic; go slowly and carefully. And stop the second you're not sure and seek reassurance by re-reading this book or getting advice from others. DIY isn't like asking for directions, you're not lost; you just need some specific info to help you out of an unfamiliar situation. There's never any shame in asking for that.

## HOW DID YOU GET ON?

You can really help other people (and me!) by leaving a review to let folks know what you thought... Plus I'll be eternally grateful and be able to write more stuff!

author.to/ian (amazon.co.uk)

amazon.com/author/iananderson (amazon.com)

goodreads.com/ian-anderson

## GETTING IN TOUCH

I'm happy to stand behind this book (and not just to avoid any eggs!). I'd be delighted to hear from you about any typos you noticed, suggestions for revisions or even   just insults or general mudslinging...

I'm always open to feedback and I love constructive criticism. I've taught myself to publish these books, so any errors you see are definitely my own.

If you're a spammer though, or overly rude, I'll have my men track you down...

You can email me at ian@handycrowd.com, or catch up with me on most flavours of social media...

facebook.com/handycrowd

twitter.com/handycrowd

pinterest.com/handycrowd

google.com/+handycrowd

YouTube.com/c/handycrowd

linkedin.com/in/ianmanderson

## COMPANION WEBSITE

You'll also find me pottering about on handycrowd.com where I'll be writing 'how to' articles and answering your emails or comments. You can subscribe for updates too. Come on in, I'll go and put the kettle on...

Stay well and I wish you well in all your own endeavours.

# OTHER WORK...

This is a different kind of DIY book. Gone are the typical (and often patronising) step-by-step instructions, and instead I've dived deep into my own head to get down on paper exactly what it is I do every day. I'll show you how to look at the world with practical eyes and how to learn just enough to get the job done.

Over 400 pages of real advice, plus tips and tricks learned from over 30 years of working on the tools every day. So stop faking it, and actually make it, be handy, live a more practical life. Start your journey at an amazon store near you...

---

Let's be honest here, home maintenance has a huge image problem. It's not cool, it's not sexy and it definitely isn't ever going to beat the thrill of building something new and shiny, not ever...

But guess what; you know that new and shiny thing you're building? Yup, it's going to need maintaining to keep it looking new and shiny.

So relax a little, surrender to it, and since you can't truly escape it anyway, let a little maintenance creep into your life. Your stuff will love you for it; you will love your stuff for looking so good, and oh; the planet will quite like you for it too. So, let me talk you into doing a little gentle home maintenance...

# RESOURCES

## LIME AND TRADITIONAL MATERIALS

www.spab.org.uk/downloads/Courses 2011/Lime Plastering Article.pdf (spaces in URL needed). A great and simple 'how to lime plaster' from Tim Tatcliffe at SPAB.

en.wikipedia.org/wiki/Lath and plaster. A little bit of wiki history about lath and plaster.

www.periodproperty.co.uk/shop/acatalog/plastering with lime.html. Find a great guide to using traditional materials here.

www.buildingconservation.com/articles/plaster/lime-plaster.htm. Popular misconceptions about traditional lime plasters are debunked here.

www.buildingconservation.com/articles/limehair/limehair.htm. Great article about the use of hair in lime plasters for reinforcement

www.buildingconservation.com/articles/internal-limeplast/internallimeplast.htm. Good descriptive article on how to use lime plaster.

www.buildingconservation.com/articles/lime-plaster-ceilings/lime-plaster-ceilings.htm Good article on ceiling defects.

www.mikewye.co.uk/guidesheets/plastering-onto-lath/. Good video showing how to plaster onto lath (and lots of other lime based videos too).

www.oldhouseonline.com/how-to-fix-plaster-ceilings/. Explains the gluing method of restoring old lath and plaster ceilings.

www.limestuff.co.uk/pages/user-guides/how-to-lime-plaster-onto-laths.html. Wiltshire based educator and supplier of lime products.

www.oldhousestore.co.uk/. Lime specialist site with some great resources about lime plus of course supplies.

www.lincolnshirelime.co.uk/. Lincolnshire based supplier of lime products.

www.bleaklow.co.uk/. Derbyshire based supplier of lime products.

www.ecolime.co.uk/. Yorkshire based supplier of lime products.

www.donhead.com/default.htm. Books about lime and conservation etc.

www.womersleys.co.uk/. Yorkshire based educator and supplier of lime products.

www.mikewye.co.uk/. Devon based educator and supplier of lime products.


## DRYWALL

en.wikipedia.org/wiki/Drywall. A little bit of wiki history about drywall.

www.familyhandyman.com/drywall/installation/how-to-hang-drywall-like-a-pro/. How to hang drywall.

www.familyhandyman.com/drywall/taping/drywall-taping-tips/view-all. Drywall tips and tricks.

www.finehomebuilding.com/how-to/tips/invisible-drywall-butt-joints.aspx Great tip to make drywall butt joints easy and invisible using flying joints.

www.british-gypsum.com/. Manufacturer of drywall products and trainer for the trade.

www.knauf.co.uk/systems/drywall-systems. Manufacturer of drywall products and trainer for the trade.

www.siniat.co.uk/. Formerly Lafarge. Manufacturer of drywall products and trainer for the trade.

## ORGANISATIONS

www.spab.org.uk/. SPAB The Society for the Protection of Ancient Buildings (and not so ancient!). These guys are superstars. Very knowledgeable advice from some very helpful folks.

www.buildingconservation.com/. Compiles the Building Conservation Directly and many useful, practical articles.

www.buildinglimesforum.org.uk/. Much more than a forum, a place to learn about lime and also get help with specific questions you may have.

www.heritage-house.org/. Everything you need to know about why you shouldn't use modern materials in your old house. Be warned, it is refreshingly honest! Work with, not against your house.

www.historicengland.org.uk/advice/your-home/. Passionate about preserving Britain's historic fabric. Help and advice about your home.

www.periodproperty.co.uk/. This sneaks on to the bottom of this list because it's really linked to the 'old house store' but it does have some useful into and a live forum.

# ABOUT THE AUTHOR

I'm an English builder who's been self-employed since the age of 18. College led to a prize or two for my skills with a trowel and now I'm a Licentiate member of the City and Guilds Institute of London. I've been called a 'good builder' and that's good enough for me...

I've built new houses; restored period houses working with perfect lime mortar and added extensions of various complexity. Plus of course maintenance on a diverse bunch of houses and commercial properties over the past 30 years.

I'm also a keen humanitarian, having worked in Uganda, teaching local artisans, building many health units in remote areas. In 2007, I helped set up projects in Rwanda for David Cameron's Department for International Development to strengthen relationships between our two countries.

I studied at the University of Lincoln gaining a Master's degree in Trauma and Disaster Management Studies to better understand some of the wider issues in developing countries.

To balance things out, I was also a househusband, looking after 3 acres of New Zealand scrub, plus of course my Norwegian wife, two fantastic children and a few crazy chickens.

I'm a 'try anything' handyman, aiming to learn something new every day. Now writing, developing products and webmastering, close to the beach in Norway, with another house project and yet more chickens...

And yes you're right, of course; the days are never long enough.

Ian Anderson MSc LCGI

# INDEX

Made in the USA
Middletown, DE
04 July 2022

68419885R00070